Tyndale Old Testament Commentaries

Volume 18

TOTC

Ecclesiastes

To the memory of my nephew,
Jomo Faal-Thomas (1988–2009).
(Ecclesiastes 3:12–14)

Tyndale Old Testament Commentaries

Volume 18

Series Editor: David G. Firth
Consulting Editor: Tremper Longman III

Ecclesiastes

An Introduction and Commentary

Knut Martin Heim

An imprint of InterVarsity Press
Downers Grove, Illinois

Inter-Varsity Press, England
36 Causton Street, London SW1P 4ST, England
Website: www.ivpbooks.com
Email: ivp@ivpbooks.com

InterVarsity Press, USA
P.O. Box 1400, Downers Grove, IL 60515, USA
Website: www.ivpress.com
Email: email@ivpress.com

Inter-Varsity Press, England, publishes Christian books that are true to the Bible and that
communicate the gospel, develop discipleship and strengthen the church for its mission in the world.

IVP originated within the Inter-Varsity Fellowship, now the Universities and Colleges Christian
Fellowship, a student movement connecting Christian Unions in universities and colleges throughout
Great Britain, and a member movement of the International Fellowship of Evangelical Students.
That historic association is maintained, and all senior IVP staff and committee members subscribe
to the UCCF Basis of Faith. Website: www.uccf.org.uk.

InterVarsity Press®, USA, is the book-publishing division of InterVarsity Christian Fellowship/
USA® and a member movement of the International Fellowship of Evangelical Students. Website:
www.intervarsity.org.

Unless otherwise stated, Scripture quotations are the author's own translation.

First published 2019

Set in Garamond 11/13pt
Typeset in Great Britain by CRB Associates, Potterhanworth, Lincolnshire
Printed and bound in Great Britain by Ashford Colour Press Ltd, Gosport, Hampshire

UK ISBN: 978-1-78359-670-6 (print)
UK ISBN: 978-1-78359-671-3 (digital)

US ISBN: 978-0-8308-4265-0 (print)
US ISBN: 978-0-8308-5076-1 (digital)

British Library Cataloguing-in-Publication Data
A catalogue record for this book is available from the British Library.

Library of Congress Cataloging-in-Publication Data
A catalog record for this book is available from the Library of Congress.

CONTENTS

GENERAL PREFACE

The decision to completely revise the Tyndale Old Testament Commentaries is an indication of the important role that the series has played since its opening volumes were released in the mid-1960s. They represented at that time, and have continued to represent, commentary writing that was committed both to the importance of the text of the Bible as Scripture and a desire to engage with as full a range of interpretive issues as possible without being lost in the minutiae of scholarly debate. The commentaries aimed to explain the biblical text to a generation of readers confronting models of critical scholarship and new discoveries from the Ancient Near East while remembering that the Old Testament is not simply another text from the ancient world. Although no uniform process of exegesis was required, all the original contributors were united in their conviction that the Old Testament remains the word of God for us today. That the original volumes fulfilled this role is evident from the way in which they continue to be used in so many parts of the world.

A crucial element of the original series was that it should offer an up-to-date reading of the text, and it is precisely for this reason that new volumes are required. The questions confronting readers in the first half of the twenty-first century are not necessarily those from the second half of the twentieth. Discoveries from the Ancient Near East continue to shed new light on the Old Testament, whilst emphases in exegesis have changed markedly. Whilst remaining true to the goals of the initial volumes, the need for contemporary study of the text requires that the series as a whole be updated. This updating is not simply a matter of commissioning new volumes to replace the old. We have also taken the opportunity to update the format of the series to reflect a key emphasis from linguistics, which is that texts communicate in larger blocks rather than in shorter segments such as individual verses. Because of this, the treatment of each section of the text includes three segments. First, a short note on *Context* is offered, placing the passage under consideration in its literary setting within the book as well as noting any historical issues crucial to interpretation. The *Comment* segment then follows the traditional structure of the commentary, offering exegesis of the various components of a passage. Finally, a brief comment is made on *Meaning*, by which is meant the message that the passage seeks to communicate within the book, highlighting its key theological themes. This section brings together the detail of the *Comment* to show how the passage under consideration seeks to communicate as a whole.

Our prayer is that these new volumes will continue the rich heritage of the Tyndale Old Testament Commentaries and that they will continue to witness to the God who is made known in the text.

David G. Firth, Series Editor
Tremper Longman III, Consulting Editor

AUTHOR'S PREFACE

My fascination with Ecclesiastes began during my studies at the Freie Theologische Akademie, Giessen, in 1986. The lectures of Dr Richard L. Schultz (now at Wheaton College) on Ecclesiastes changed my theology and my life, and he has been a friend and encourager ever since. I am grateful for the sabbatical granted by Trinity College Bristol in 2015, during which much of the groundwork for this commentary was laid. One of the key aspects of Ecclesiastes that struck me at that time was the *underdetermined* nature of its language.

Many thanks are also due to colleagues and friends at Denver Seminary, Colorado. Here I had the opportunity to present lectures on Ecclesiastes in the Spring semesters of 2017 and 2018, during which much of the substance of the commentary took shape. My Old Testament colleagues Dr Hélène M. Dallaire and Dr Richard S. Hess provided thought-provoking advice and asked insightful questions which helped me to refine my approach to the book. Special thanks are also due to Revd Peter Heim and his wife Dr Erin Heim, who invited me to a show by stand-up comedian Jim Gaffigan. Attending this show had a profound impact on this commentary.

In week five of the Spring semester of 2018, while preparing the lecture on Ecclesiastes 5 for that week, I read Thomas Krüger's comments on Ecclesiastes 5:8–9 (5:7–8 in Hebrew) in his *Qoheleth* commentary in the Hermeneia series. He highlighted how verse 8 can be read both as a defence and as a radical critique of governmental organization. His observations also helped me to discover the progression from *intentional ambiguity* in verse 8 to *calculated hyper-ambiguity* in verse 9, because here the monarch is mentioned, in a statement that can also be read both as a defence and as a radical critique. It was at this point that I first understood the purpose of *underdetermination* in the language of Ecclesiastes. It created *plausible deniability* in case the book's regime-critical potential were discovered by those it aimed to critique.

From here, the link via Jim Gaffigan to the humorous regime-critical routines of modern stand-up comedians under repressive regimes was a natural one, for here, too, underdetermined language provides plausible deniability to hide risky regime-critical comment. For the remainder of the semester, I began to interpret the book through this lens, paying special attention to underdetermination, regime-critical potential and humour. To my surprise, these could be found almost everywhere. I am grateful to the students in the class who, while initially sceptical, asked great questions and offered many constructive observations that helped me refine my approach.

By the end of the semester, I had become convinced that the book as we now have it is the written record of a speech sequence similar to the routines of modern stand-up comedians, who use the medium of comedy to critique problematic issues, an insight which made it necessary to rewrite the commentary in its entirety. I am grateful to Tyndale Old Testament Commentaries Series Editor Dr David Firth and to Dr Philip Duce at Inter-Varsity Press for their help. Ultimate gratitude goes to the God who inspired the book of Ecclesiastes and helped me to understand it in a fresh way. Soli Deo gloria.

Knut M. Heim
Denver Seminary, Littleton

ABBREVIATIONS

Bible versions

GNB The Good News Bible published by The Bible Societies/
HarperCollins Publishers Ltd UK, copyright ©
American Bible Society, 1966, 1971, 1976, 1992, 1994.

MT Masoretic Text

NIV The Holy Bible, New International Version (Anglicized
edition). Copyright © 1979, 1984, 2011 by Biblica. Used
by permission of Hodder & Stoughton Ltd, an Hachette
UK company. All rights reserved. 'NIV' is a registered
trademark of Biblica. UK trademark number 1448790.

NRSV The New Revised Standard Version of the Bible,
Anglicized Edition, copyright © 1989, 1995 by the
Division of Christian Education of the National Council
of the Churches of Christ in the USA. Used by
permission. All rights reserved.

SELECT BIBLIOGRAPHY

Bartholomew, C. G. (2009), *Ecclesiastes* (Grand Rapids: Baker Academic).

—— (2014), 'The Intertextuality of Ecclesiastes and the New Testament', in K. J. Dell and W. Kynes (eds.), *Reading Ecclesiastes Intertextually* (London: Bloomsbury T&T Clark), 226–239.

Barton, G. A. (1908), *A Critical and Exegetical Commentary on the Book of Ecclesiastes* (Edinburgh: T&T Clark).

Brown, L. (ed.) (1993), *New Shorter Oxford English Dictionary on Historical Principles*, vol. 1: A – M (Oxford: Clarendon Press).

Budge, E. A. W. (1968), *Egypt under the Saïtes, Persians, and Ptolemies* (Oosterhout: Anthropological Publications).

Childs, B. S. (1979), *Introduction to the Old Testament as Scripture* (London: SCM).

Crenshaw, J. L. (1987), *Ecclesiastes: A Commentary* (Philadelphia: Westminster Press).

—— (2005), 'Ecclesiastes', *Interpretation* 59: 192–194.

Crüsemann, F. (1984), 'The Unchangeable World: The "Crisis of Wisdom" in Koheleth', in W. Schottroff and W. Stegemann (eds.), *God of the Lowly: Socio-Historical Interpretations of the Bible* (Maryknoll: Orbis), 57–77.

Delitzsch, F. (1975), *Proverbs, Ecclesiastes, Song of Solomon* (Grand Rapids: Eerdmans).

Dell, K. J., and W. Kynes (2014), *Reading Ecclesiastes Intertextually* (London: Bloomsbury T&T Clark).

Eaton, M. A. (1983), *Ecclesiastes: An Introduction and Commentary* (Leicester: Inter-Varsity Press; Downers Grove: InterVarsity Press).

Ehrlich, A. B. (1968), *Randglossen zur hebräischen Bibel* (Hildesheim: Olms).

Enns, P. (2011), *Ecclesiastes* (Grand Rapids: Eerdmans).

Fox, M. V. (1988), 'Aging and Death in Qohelet 12', *Journal for the Study of the Old Testament* 13: 55–77.

—— (1989), *Qohelet and His Contradictions* (Decatur, GA: Almond Press).

—— (1999), *A Time to Tear Down and a Time to Build Up: A Rereading of Ecclesiastes* (Grand Rapids: Eerdmans).

—— (2004), *Ecclesiastes: The Traditional Hebrew Text with the New JPS Translation* (Philadelphia: Jewish Publication Society).

Gafni, I. (2008), 'Gymnasium', in *Encyclopedia Judaica* (New York: Macmillan), 160–161.

Gordis, R. (1968), *Koheleth, the Man and His World: A Study of Ecclesiastes* (New York: Schocken Books).

Graetz, H. (1998), *Geschichte der Juden: Von den ältesten Zeiten bis in die Gegenwart*, vol. 2/2 (Darmstadt: Wissenschaftliche Buchgesellschaft).

Hays, D. J. (2003), 'Has the Narrator Come to Praise Solomon or Bury Him? Narrative Subtlety in 1 Kings 1 – 11', *Journal for the Study of the Old Testament* 28: 149–174.

Hengstenberg, E. W. (1869), *A Commentary on Ecclesiastes* (Evansville, IN: Sovereign Grace).

Hess, R. D. (2016), *The Old Testament: A Historical, Theological, and Critical Introduction* (Grand Rapids: Baker Academic).

Hodel-Hoenes, S. (1991), *Leben und Tod im alten Ägypten: Thebanische Privatgräber des neuen Reiches* (Darmstadt: Wissenschaftliche Buchgesellschaft).

Horace (2012), *Odes*, Book 1, ed. Roland Mayer (Cambridge/ New York: Cambridge University Press).

Ingram, D. (2006), *Ambiguity in Ecclesiastes* (New York: T&T Clark International).

Izard, C. E. (2009), 'Despair', in D. Sander and K. R. Scherer (eds.), *The Oxford Companion to Emotion and the Affective Sciences* (Oxford: Oxford University Press), 116–117.

Jarick, J. (2014), 'Ecclesiastes among the Comedians', in K. J. Dell and W. Kynes (eds.), *Reading Ecclesiastes Intertextually* (London: Bloomsbury T&T Clark), 176–188.

Koehler, L., W. Baumgartner and J. J. Stamm (2001), *The Hebrew and Aramaic Lexicon of the Old Testament* (Leiden: Brill).

Koh, Y. V. (2006), 'Royal Autobiography in the Book of Qoheleth', PhD thesis, Faculty of Oriental Studies, University of Cambridge.

Krüger, T. (2004), *Qoheleth: A Commentary* (Minneapolis: Fortress).

Kushner, H. S. (1981), *When Bad Things Happen to Good People* (New York: Schocken Books).

Lauha, A. (1978), *Kohelet* (Neukirchen-Vluyn: Neukirchener Verlag).

Limburg, J. (2006), *Encountering Ecclesiastes: A Book for Our Time* (Grand Rapids: Eerdmans).

Loader, J. A. (1986), *Ecclesiastes: A Practical Commentary* (Grand Rapids: Eerdmans).

Lohfink, N. (1981), '*Melek, šallît* und *môšēl* bei Kohelet und die Abfassungszeit des Buches', *Biblica* 62: 535–543.

—— (1994), 'Grenzen und Einbindung des Kohelet-Schlussgedichts', in P. Mommer and W. Thiel (eds.), *Altes Testament – Forschung und Wirkung: Festschrift für Henning Graf Reventlow* (Frankfurt: Lang), 33–46.

—— (2003), *Qoheleth: A Continental Commentary* (Minneapolis: Fortress).

Longman III, T. (1998), *The Book of Ecclesiastes* (Grand Rapids: Eerdmans).

Loretz, O. (1964), *Qohelet und der Alte Orient: Untersuchungen zu Stil und theologischer Thematik des Buches Qohelet* (Freiburg: Herder).

Lyubomirsky, S., and J. L. Kurtz (2009), 'Happiness', in D. Sander and K. R. Scherer (eds.), *The Oxford Companion to Emotion and the Affective Sciences* (Oxford: Oxford University Press), 203.

McDiarmid, I. (2008), 'Underdetermination and Indeterminacy: What Is the Difference?', *Erkenntnis* 69: 279–293.

Meek, R. L. (2016), 'Twentieth- and Twenty-First-Century Readings of Hebel (הֶבֶל) in Ecclesiastes', *Currents in Biblical Research* 14: 279–297.

Murphy, R. E. (1992), *Ecclesiastes* (Dallas: Word).

Ogden, G. S. (1984), 'Qoheleth XI 7 – XII 8: Qoheleth's Summons to Enjoyment and Reflection', *Vetus Testamentum* 34: 27–38.

—— (1987), *Qoheleth* (Sheffield: JSOT Press).

Plumptre, E. H. (1898), *Ecclesiastes*, Cambridge Bible for Schools and Colleges (Cambridge: Cambridge University Press).

Provan, I. W. (2001), *Ecclesiastes, Song of Songs: From Biblical Text . . . to Contemporary Life*, NIV Application Commentary (Grand Rapids: Zondervan).

Ringgren, H., and W. Zimmerli (1981), *Sprüche, Prediger, Das Hohe Lied, Klagelieder, Das Buch Esther* (Göttingen: Vandenhoeck & Ruprecht).

Schroeder, T. (2009), 'Introspection', in D. Sander and K. R. Scherer (eds.), *The Oxford Companion to Emotion and the Affective Sciences* (Oxford: Oxford University Press), 226.

Schroer, S., and T. Stäubli (2001), *Body Symbolism in the Bible* (Collegeville: Liturgical Press).

Seow, C. L. (1997), *Ecclesiastes: A New Translation with Introduction and Commentary* (New York: Doubleday).

—— (2001), 'Theology When Everything Is Out of Control', *Interpretation* 55: 237–249.

Smith, M. S. (2010), *God in Translation: Deities in Cross-Cultural Discourse* (Grand Rapids: Eerdmans).

Tamez, E. (2000), *When the Horizons Close: Rereading Ecclesiastes* (Maryknoll: Orbis).

Thiselton, A. C. (1992), *New Horizons in Hermeneutics* (London: HarperCollins).

van Dijk, W. W. (2009), 'Disappointment', in D. Sander and K. R. Scherer (eds.), *The Oxford Companion to Emotion and the Affective Sciences* (Oxford: Oxford University Press), 120–121.

Waltke, B. K., and M. O'Connor (1990), *An Introduction to Biblical Hebrew Syntax* (Winona Lake: Eisenbrauns).

Weeks, S. (2012), *Ecclesiastes and Scepticism* (New York: T&T Clark International).

Whitley, C. F. (1979), *Koheleth: His Language and Thought* (Berlin/ New York: de Gruyter).

Whybray, R. N. (1982), 'Qoheleth, Preacher of Joy', *Journal for the Study of the Old Testament* 7: 87–98.

—— (1989), *Ecclesiastes: Based on the Revised Standard Version* (Grand Rapids: Eerdmans).

Wolff, H. W. (1974), *Anthropology of the Old Testament* (London: SCM).

INTRODUCTION

1. Title and authorship

In the title of the book, its author is described as *son of David* and *king in Jerusalem*. This suggests Solomon, but the alias *Qoheleth* suggests an anonymous 'royal' figure from the line of David whose name and actual identity are deliberately obscured. This would have been obvious to the live audiences who attended Qoheleth's oral performances, while later readers of the book soon neglected the pseudonym and latched on to the royal aspects of his description. The debate over the identity of the author of the book of Ecclesiastes is thus a recent one. From antiquity until the eighteenth century, virtually everybody assumed that the author was Solomon, the son of David, who was king over all Israel in Jerusalem from 971 to 931 BC. This virtual unanimity is surprising because the author is not named as Solomon, in contrast with the titles of Proverbs and Song of Songs. Very few scholars today still support Solomonic authorship, on the basis that 1:1 and 1:12 – 2:26 are most naturally read this way (Longman 1998: 3). Such arguments overlook the rhetorical and ironical quality of these statements, which this commentary will demonstrate. Furthermore, the language of the book belongs to a later stage in Israel's history, well after the exile (Delitzsch 1975: 190), and any allusions to or similarities with Solomon end after chapter 2, while passages that do refer to kingship later in the book (e.g. 4:1–3; 5:8–9; 8:2–9; 10:20) are critical of royalty.

The word 'Qoheleth' is a Qal feminine participle of the verb *qhl*, which means 'to assemble'. The noun *qāhāl* means 'assembly'. 'Qoheleth' appears only in this book, and its particular form, a feminine singular participle, identifies his professional or well-established social role as a speaker at group gatherings. The designation is an overtly fictitious name, a pseudonym (Longman 1998: 4) to ensure the speaker's anonymity.

The designation is thus used both as the orator's nickname and as his professional title, just as a professional smith in English is sometimes called 'Smithy', as if that were his name (*Qoheleth*, 1:1, 2, 12; 7:27; 12:9, 10), and sometimes referred to as 'the smith', using the title for his profession (*the qoheleth*; only in 12:8). This commentary will use that designation throughout in order to reflect its pseudonymous character. All the explicit statements about Qoheleth's activities describe him performing the contents of the book in spoken format. Qoheleth's speech begins and ends with his motto (*everything is a mirage*) in 1:2 (*says Qoheleth*) and 12:8 (*says the qoheleth*), supplemented with an appendix by a later editor who evaluates and recommends the work to a later generation of readers (12:9–14).

2. Intertextual issues

The book of Ecclesiastes shares themes with a very wide variety of texts from the ancient world. A convenient compendium of essays exploring the book's intertextual relations is a 2014 volume entitled *Reading Ecclesiastes Intertextually* (Dell and Kynes 2014).

Of particular interest is an essay by John Jarick (Jarick 2014). Setting aside questions of familiarity and dependence, he presents a comparison between similar statements in Ecclesiastes and several Greek comic poets, especially Aristophanes and Menander.

Picking up on the editorial note regarding Qoheleth's *pleasing words* (12:10), rendered 'words of pleasure' by Jarick, he demonstrates that many of Qoheleth's pronouncements may have 'a certain comedic hue', that they 'can be seen to chime with notes struck in the Athenian theatre'. In consequence, he concludes, '[p]erhaps reading Ecclesiastes alongside the comic poets of ancient Greece really can bring a different perspective to bear on the supposedly world-weary aspect of the book' (Jarick 2014: 187). His comparison may indeed 'encourage readers to hear Ecclesiastes' pessimistic ponderings differently, as the similarities in theme, imagery and language with the Greek comedians cause that ancient laughter to echo in their ears' (Jarick 2014: 177). Jarick's comparison lends weight to the interpretation of the book of Ecclesiastes as political satire presented in the present commentary.

3. Canonical significance

The book of Ecclesiastes took pride of place in the discussions of the Council of Jamnia in AD 90. The dispute over its status as sacred scripture concerned its apparently 'secular' character, apparent internal contradictions, and statements which seemed to promote heretical thought, such as 1:3 and 11:9. The circumstance that a manuscript of Ecclesiastes was found among the Dead Sea Scrolls discovered at Qumran suggests that the community who treasured these texts considered Ecclesiastes to be authoritative well before the Christian era (Bartholomew 2009: 19–20).

Despite its canonical status, Christians have struggled with how the book could be useful for them. This struggle is already in view from earliest times, as the rarity of references or allusions to Ecclesiastes in the New Testament reveals. The only possible quotation appears in Romans 3:10, which appears to reference Ecclesiastes 7:20. Possible allusions include Romans 1:21 and 8:20, where the word 'futility' is the same word *mataiotēs* which the Septuagint uses to translate *hebel*. The contrast between the wisdom of God and the wisdom of the world in 1 Corinthians 1:20–22 may also have been inspired by the critique of wisdom in Ecclesiastes (Childs 1979: 588). In a fascinating and theologically rich essay, Bartholomew explores the broader *intertextual* relations between

Ecclesiastes and the New Testament, but this does not compensate for the fact that Ecclesiastes is one of the least quoted Old Testament texts in the New Testament (Bartholomew 2014). In more recent times, doubts over the relevance of Ecclesiastes for Christians has continued (Thiselton 1992: 65–66; Bartholomew 2009: 20). Richard Hess considers the book a possible stepping stone towards faith (Hess 2016: 492–493).

I agree with Hess. There is no doubt that the book has functioned in this manner for many, not only for those who have encountered the Christian faith for the first time, but also for those who have discovered that a more simplistic and naïve kind of faith in which they grew up does not prove true to reality. Ecclesiastes can and does indeed function in this way at the level of its non-subversive 'official' meaning.

Beyond this, however, there is also a second meaning, as the detailed comments on one passage after another will demonstrate. This hidden and subversive meaning appeals to the community of faith in Qoheleth's time. It combines with the 'official' meaning to produce a message that is rich in theological meaning, has the capacity to strengthen its readers' faith in the midst of adversity and proves enormously fruitful for practical Christian living today. We will explore this potential of the book as we consider the *Meaning* of each part of Qoheleth's speech.

4. Date and historical context

The language of the book, which reflects all the characteristics of Late Biblical Hebrew, as well as numerous references to sociopolitical circumstances which best fit that time, provide persuasive evidence that the speech was composed in Jerusalem in the final decades of the third century BC. For these reasons, this is the majority position of recent commentators (Krüger 2004: 19–21). Qoheleth's use of the phrase *under the sun* as a cypher for foreign rule under Egypt, demonstrated in the next part of this introduction, offers further evidence to this effect. The political context to which the book responds is a period of foreign rule over Judea under the Ptolemaic Dynasty of Greek rulers in Egypt.

5. Language and style, genres and intention

The book of Ecclesiastes has received very different interpretations. The reason for this phenomenon lies in the fascinating
nature of the book itself. Much in the book is calculatedly
ambiguous (Ingram 2006, 2013). The book's contents were produced during the explosive sociopolitical circumstances under
foreign rule exercised by the Greek Ptolemaic kings in Egypt.
The apparent superiority of the Greeks was very attractive to the
Jewish population, many of whom began to adopt Greek values
and habits (Graetz 1998: 197–266). Hidden references to current
events, a clandestine form of humour and the oral character of his
composition explain the underdetermined nature of Qoheleth's
language and reveal the subversively sociocritical intent behind
his work.

The strategies of indirection which Qoheleth employs have
in more recent times been most prominent among stand-up
comedians active in countries with politically repressive regimes.
In their routines, comedians make veiled allusions to current affairs
which are specific enough for the insider audience to recognize the
reference to real-life events while carefully concealing what the talk
is really about behind underdetermined language. Good examples
in Ecclesiastes are the phrase *under the sun* as a cypher for Egyptian
rule and the allusion to religious provocation and its violent consequences in 8:10–14.

The designation 'underdetermination' is normally used in the
philosophy of science. In complex scientific theories, such as
general relativity or quantum mechanics, different theories can be
supported by the same evidence (McDiarmid 2008). I have coined
the designation 'underdetermined language' to describe the kinds
of expressions that result from the *strategies of indirection* employed
by Qoheleth and many modern stand-up comedians, where the
language is intentionally vague so that it will be understood in
different ways because information that would fix the meaning
of such expressions is purposefully suppressed in order to create
plausible deniability.

Like the routines of many stand-up comedians, Qoheleth helps
his audience to laugh about the foreign occupiers and about

themselves. We are dealing with political satire. The book of Ecclesiastes is resistance literature.

Three prominent phrases in Qoheleth's oratory – the catchphrase
under the sun, the buzzword *success* and the metaphor *hebel*, translated
mirage in this commentary – illustrate the subversive nature of the
book.

Under the sun (taḥat haššemeš). The phrase initially appears to be a
reference to 'life on earth' or 'the universality of human experience'. Against the historical background of foreign rule under
the Egyptian Ptolemaic kings, however, the phrase is also a cypher
for Egypt: it means 'subject to the Egyptian foreign regime'. The
following arguments support this conclusion: (1) The title 'the Sun'
was a common epithet for the Egyptian pharaohs who, as head of
state, represented Egyptian rule, at home and abroad. Cross-
cultural correspondence addressed to the Egyptian pharaoh
regularly names the monarch as 'the Sun' (Smith 2010: 66).[1] (2) The
Ptolemaic kings carried the designation 'son of the Sun' in their
official throne cartouches (Budge 1968: 179). (3) All Ptolemies
assumed the identity of and were worshipped as gods. (4) A likely
objection to this argument is in fact evidence in its favour. Similar
expressions, like the phrase *under the heavens* – which in Qoheleth
clearly seems to refer to the same entity as *under the sun* – may refer
to nothing else but 'life on earth'. In response, an innocuous alternative formulation like *under the heavens* creates plausible deniability.
(5) These arguments do not prove that the phrase is a cypher for
Egyptian rule over Judea, and this is precisely the point. Qoheleth
had to be careful, and this is why his oratory is so multivalent.

Success (yitrôn). The expression was a buzzword trending among
Qoheleth's audience, which explains why there was no need for
him to explain it. A neologism coined among Hellenizing Jews
to express their aspirations to take advantage of the new opportunities, it meant to express economic and social success in the
pursuit of personal happiness, something which, according to

---

1. The letters from El Amarna date from a much earlier period, but they
are reflective of an enduring literary tradition. The relative distance
also aids the cause of plausible deniability.

the foreign worldview, seemed obtainable without observance of the Jewish religion, as a natural reward for hard work. In response, Qoheleth carries out a thorough search for *success* through human effort. In the process, his inquiry demonstrates that the *success* which his target audience seeks without the Jewish God is unobtainable.

Mirage (hebel). The word *hebel* occurs seventy-three times in the Hebrew Bible, thirty-eight times in Ecclesiastes. It also appears as Abel's name in Genesis 4:2, where it implies how ephemeral, transient and vulnerable human life and endeavour are in the face of sin (Hess 2016: 484). According to a standard dictionary, it carries three meanings: (1) 'breath'; (2) 'vanity'; (3) 'idols, things that do not really exist' (Koehler, Baumgartner and Stamm 2001: 236). The first of these proposed paraphrases correctly expresses one specific meaning of the word, but fails to recognize that the term refers to bodies of warm air in general, and so includes similar phenomena such as mist, fog and other kinds of vapour. The second paraphrase is an incorrect *interpretation* of the word first proposed by Jerome (Meek 2016). And the third paraphrase confuses a metaphor to describe idols with the referents of that metaphor, namely idols.

In reality, the word normally refers to warm air, briefly visible as water molecules contained in it condense when it cools. A larger body of warm air, such as mist, can remain visible for a longer time. It is a visual metaphor. Mist appears to be more substantial than it is (ephemerality), soon disappears (transience) and hides objects behind it, obscuring reality from view (illusoriness). All of these aspects of mist are especially prominent in a metaphorical use of the word *hebel*: its usage to describe the optical phenomenon of 'mirages'. The *New Shorter Oxford English Dictionary* defines mirages as 'an optical illusion caused by atmospheric conditions' through the refraction of light in hot air, giving the following example: 'the false appearance of a distant sheet of water in a desert'. Figuratively, the word 'mirage' can also mean 'an illusion, a fantasy' (Brown 1993: 1785). The majority of the occurrences of the word *hebel* in the Old Testament carry the meaning 'mirage', referring either to an optical illusion or to an illusion in general. In Ecclesiastes, all occurrences of the word *hebel* refer to an illusion.

These three prominent expressions in Qoheleth's oratory – the catchphrase *under the sun* (*taḥat haššemeš*), the buzzword *success* (*yitrôn*) and the metaphor *hebel*, translated *mirage* in this commentary – not only illustrate the subversive nature of the book, they also reveal the purpose of Qoheleth's entire speech, namely to motivate his contemporaries to remain faithful to their God and their trad-itional cultural values.

The book of Ecclesiastes is the written record of a speech that has been composed and performed by a poetic prophet. Qoheleth was *the qoheleth* (12:8), an accomplished public orator who employed his formidable skills in an explosive amalgam of rhetorical schemes and devices borrowed from the traditional arsenals of Hebrew eloquence and Greek rhetoric. His sharp tongue combined these rhetorical weapons in a new way to fight a guerrilla war of the mind. With 4,170 words in the 222 verses of the book, a performance of the whole would have lasted about forty minutes.

6. Theological and practical message

Opinions on the theology of the book of Ecclesiastes differ wildly. On the one hand, a significant minority opinion maintains that the book's protagonist is an orthodox teacher with a positive view of life (see the literature listed in Longman 1998: 31 n. 119). On the other hand, a strong majority position advocates that Qoheleth is a disillusioned sceptic who challenges orthodox beliefs. 'Commen-tators remain polarized as to whether Ecclesiastes is fundamentally positive, affirming joy, or basically pessimistic' (Bartholomew 2009: 93). The interpretation of Ecclesiastes as resistance literature in the form of political satire resolves this scholarly impasse.

a. The practical message of Ecclesiastes
The sociopolitical situation of the Jewish struggle for the survival of their socioreligious identity under foreign rule leads to a rhet-orical strategy that fully affirms the illusory nature of life *under the sun*, that is, under foreign rule, while at the same time promoting a positive, hopeful outlook on life conducted within the trajectory of Jewish religion and tradition.

Qoheleth's instruction operates on two levels of meaning. On the surface level, he presents a theoretical debate on the purpose of life. On a deeper level of meaning, he aims to subvert the corrupting influence of foreign rule.

For those in the know, then, his message is not an abstract, disembodied philosophical tract, but one that is deeply rooted in their own painful experience under foreign rule. It is a missive of hope, a rallying cry to cultural resistance, an appeal to remain faithful to their God.

b. The portrayal of God in Ecclesiastes

God the giver. God gives the ability to enjoy the good things of ordinary life (2:24–25; 3:13), he gives wisdom and joy (2:26) and he redistributes material goods from sinners to the righteous (2:26). He gives challenging tasks to human beings (3:10–11). God has predetermined (given) the lifespan of human beings (5:18). God grants resources for enjoyment and enables contentment with constraint of ambitions and enjoyment of labour as a gift (5:19). But despite his provision of resources for human flourishing, he sometimes apparently withholds the opportunity for humans to consume these because he allows others to snatch them from their owners (6:2). God has given human beings *hard work* to do during the days of their lives *under the sun* (8:15).

The fear of God. Qoheleth counsels ethical and epistemic moderation, on the grounds that fearing God will give people the capacity to overcome obstacles. In the face of the systematic perversion of justice in his day, Qoheleth affirms his certainty that, in the long run, *it will turn out well for those who fear God* (7:17–18). By contrast, however, *it will not turn out well for the wicked . . . because he has not walked in fear before God* (8:12–13).

Qoheleth's instructions concerning God. Qoheleth's speeches include a high number of instructions on how humans should relate to God. He advises his listeners to watch their feet on the way to worship (4:17). He urges worshippers to prepare carefully what they present to God, in order to keep their public prayer in the house of worship brief (5:1). The rationale for these instructions either lies in the spatial distance between worshipper and God, or it is grounded in the different status that God and worshipper occupy in the social hierarchy (*for God is in heaven, but you are on earth*, 5:2). Those who have made a vow to God are urged to fulfil it (5:4). In circumstances where numbers of dreams, words and sensory illusions increase, the hearer is advised to fear God (5:7). Readers are also encouraged to invest in diverse ventures (11:2) because the way in which God will respond to human endeavours is as mysterious as the causes of prenatal human survival (11:5).

In a concluding and climactic series of eight instructions which present a virtual 'theology of happiness', Qoheleth urges his audience to remember that they are accountable to God not only for the wrong things they have done, but also for the good things they have not done or enjoyed in their life (11:9). The series and the entire routine conclude with the instruction that his audience should always seek to please God (12:1), and the series is given urgency with a dramatic description of impending obstacles to happiness (12:2–7), a magnificent prophetic and poetic masterpiece which brings Qoheleth's routine to a dramatically stunning theological conclusion: in the affirmation that in human death *the dust [returns] to the earth, just as it was, and the spirit [returns] to God who gave it*, God emerges as the origin and destiny of human life.

God and carpe diem.[2] God is mentioned in most of the seven *carpe diem* passages. Only in the second passage, the briefest of all (3:22), is God not mentioned. In the first passage, 2:24–26, God enables human satisfaction from the fruits of their labour (v. 24). The rhetorical question in verse 25, in fact, implies that the ability to enjoy the fruits of one's labour can come only through divine gift, a truth illustrated with the claim that God rewards *good* people with wisdom, knowledge and joy through redistributing wealth from sinners to them (v. 26). Similarly, in the third passage, 3:13 claims that any human's capacity to *eat and drink and see good in his hard work* is *a gift from God*. In the same manner, the fourth passage, 5:18–20, also claims that every human being to whom God has

---

2. The Latin phrase *carpe diem* (lit. 'seize the day') originates with the Latin poet Horace (Horace 2012). In *Odes* 1.11.8, the poet urges the reader to 'seize the day' and enjoy it rather than worry about a distant future or hope for something better in an uncertain tomorrow.

given wealth and possessions *and* whom he has enabled to enjoy them *with contentment* can do so only because that *is a gift from God* (v. 19). The fifth passage, 8:15, is somewhat different because here it is the days of people's life under the sun that God is said to have given, but even so, Qoheleth commends eating, drinking and enjoyment. In the sixth passage, 9:7–10, Qoheleth instructs his audience as follows: *Go, eat your bread with enjoyment, and drink your wine with a good conscience, for God has already approved what you do!* Paradoxically, this strongly worded affirmation of divine approval is tantalizingly tempered with a complementary statement in the seventh and final, climactic *carpe diem* passage (11:9), which belongs to the extensive series of instructions to maximize happiness in 11:8 – 12:1. Here Qoheleth reminds his audience that they are accountable to God not only for the wrong things they have done, but also for the good things they have not done or enjoyed in their lives (11:9). Against the gloomy canvas of life *under the sun*, then, God emerges as the 'giver of good gifts' *par excellence*, as the Giver of Joy, and Qoheleth as his Preacher of Joy (Whybray 1982).

ANALYSIS

1. INTRODUCTION TO A PHILOSOPHICAL TREATISE ON HUMAN LIMITATIONS AND HAPPINESS (1:1–3)

2. COMPLEXITY OF THE SEARCH FOR HAPPINESS DEMONSTRATED THROUGH POETIC MEDITATIONS ON THE CYCLICAL NATURE OF NATURAL PHENOMENA AND THE LIMITS OF HUMAN EXPERIENCE (1:4–11)

3. CASE STUDY 1, A THOUGHT EXPERIMENT: QOHELETH'S ADOPTION OF THE IDENTITY OF A SOLOMONIC CARICATURE TO EXPLORE SUCCESS THROUGH THE UNLIMITED SATISFACTION OF HUMAN DESIRES (1:12 – 2:26)

A. The preamble to the experiment (1:12–18)
B. The methodology of the experiment (2:1–3)
C. The report on the experiment (2:4–10)
D. The analysis of the experiment (2:11–16)
E. The emotional response to the experiment (2:17–23)
F. The conclusions from the experiment (2:24–26)

15. CASE STUDY 9: A SPECIFIC CAUSE OF MISERY DESPITE ABUNDANT WEALTH (6:3–9)

16. A REFLECTION ON THE HUMAN CONDITION IN THE LIGHT OF CASE STUDIES 6–9 (6:10–12)

17. FOURTH PRACTICAL INTERLUDE: INSTRUCTION ON COPING WITH BEREAVEMENT (7:1–14)

18. FIFTH PRACTICAL INTERLUDE: INSTRUCTION ON COPING WITH THE LACK OF A DIRECT CORRELATION BETWEEN ACTS AND THEIR CONSEQUENCES (7:15–22)

19. REFLECTIONS ON THE RESEARCH IMPACT OF THE PRECEDING CASE STUDIES (7:23 – 8:1)

20. FURTHER REFLECTIONS ON THE RESEARCH IMPACT OF THE PRECEDING CASE STUDIES (8:2–9)

21. FURTHER REFLECTIONS ON THE ABUSE OF POWER (8:10–14)

22. CONCLUDING REFLECTIONS ON THE ABUSE OF POWER AND THE APPARENT INCONGRUITY BETWEEN DEEDS AND THEIR CONSEQUENCES (8:15 – 9:1)

23. REFLECTION ON THE UNIVERSALITY OF DEATH, IRRESPECTIVE OF MORAL OR RELIGIOUS QUALITIES (9:2–10)

24. REFLECTION ON THE PRECARIOUS UNPREDICTABILITY OF HUMAN LIFE (9:11–12)

25. CASE STUDY 10: WISDOM WITHOUT WEALTH IGNORED (9:13 – 10:4)

TRANSLATION

My translation is semantically, grammatically and syntactically expressive, with the aim of reflecting, as much as possible, the feel of the Hebrew original. Items in square brackets supply information that is implicit in the Hebrew and necessary for understanding (e.g. 'to pleasure [I said]: "What can you achieve?"' in 2:2). Words or phrases in italics separated by a slash (e.g. 'do not be *frightened/surprised* by the matter, for one official *watches over/ watches out for* the one above him' in 5:8) identify wordplays and similar phenomena, where the Hebrew intentionally has several meanings.

¹·¹ The words of Qoheleth, son of David, king in Jerusalem.
² 'A mirage, nothing but a mirage,' says Qoheleth,
'a mirage, nothing but a mirage. It's all a mirage.'
³ What profit is there for humans in all their hard work
with which they work so hard under the sun?

⁴ A generation goes and a generation comes;
but the earth remains ever the same.
⁵ The sun rises and the sun goes down,
and hurries back to its origin,
from where it keeps rising.
⁶ Going south and turning north,
turning, turnin', going, the wind;
and to its surroundings, returns the wind.

⁷ All streams go into the sea,
but the sea never fills up;
to the place where the streams go,
there they return, in order to go again.
⁸ All these breathtaking things
humans cannot capture with words,
[. . .] the eye cannot be satisfied with seeing,
and [. . .] the ear cannot be filled with hearing.

⁹ Whatever that is, that's what will be,
and whatever has been done, that's what will be done,
and there is nothing that's entirely new under the sun.
¹⁰ Is there anything of which one can say:
'Look at this, that is new?' –
It's already been there, a long time ago;
it's something which was there before our time.
¹¹ There is no memory of former events;
and even for the events which will happen
there will be no remembrance with those who will
        be hereafter.

¹² I, Qoheleth, was king over Israel in Jerusalem.
¹³ And I set my heart on investigating and exploring by wisdom
everything that is done under the heavens – and look:
it is a dreadful task God gave humans to tackle!
¹⁴ I considered every doing that is done under the sun – and look:
everything is a mirage and a chasing after wind,
¹⁵ what is bent cannot be straightened,
and what is missing cannot be counted.
¹⁶ I spoke, I with my heart:
'I, look, I have expanded and I have added so much more wisdom
than all who have been before me over Jerusalem,
and my heart has seen an abundance of wisdom and knowledge.'
¹⁷ And I set my heart on understanding wisdom and on understanding
        foolishness – and incongruity I discovered: that even this is
        a chasing after wind!
¹⁸ For with much wisdom, much resentment;
and adding knowledge adds pain.

²:¹ I said to my heart:
'Come on, then, let me test you by pleasure,
and you, see what is good!' – and look, this too was a mirage:
² to laughter I said: 'You are to be praised,'
to pleasure [I said]: 'What can you achieve?'
³ I explored my heart
by stretching my body through wine
(all the while my heart guiding [me] by wisdom!)
and by grasping a state of irrationality
until I would see whether or not this is good for human beings
          to do under heaven [for] the number of days of their lives.

⁴ I made great my works:
I built myself houses,
I planted myself vineyards.
⁵ I made myself gardens and orchards and I planted in them fruit trees
          of every kind.
⁶ I made myself a cascade of ponds to irrigate a grove of lush trees.
⁷ I acquired servants and maidservants,
and children of a house there was for myself;
also an increasing holding of cattle and sheep there was for myself,
so many more than anyone before me in Jerusalem.
⁸ I even accumulated for myself silver and gold and the most treasured
          possessions of kings and provinces – I trained myself male and
          female singers, and what pleasures men – women with big breasts.
⁹ And I became so much greater and richer
than anyone who had been in Jerusalem before me.
(Even so, my wisdom stood by me!)
¹⁰ And nothing my eyes desired I withheld from them;
I did not deny my heart anything from all the pleasures
that my heart desired from all my hard work;
and that was my share from all my hard work.

¹¹ Then I faced all my deeds which my hands had done,
and the hard work at which I had worked so hard to do –
and look: it was all a mirage and chasing after wind,
and there was no success under the sun.
¹² And I faced to see wisdom and folly and irrationality, namely:

What will the man do who comes after the king? –
Just what they have done before!
[13] And I saw that
there is a success for wisdom over irrationality,
just as light has success over darkness;
[14] the wise has his eyes in his head,
but the fool keeps walking in darkness;
but I also discovered this:
for one destiny they are destined, all of them!
[15] And I said to my heart:
'To the same destiny as the fool I also am destined.
Why then did I behave so excessively wise?'
And I spoke to my heart:
'This also is a mirage,
[16] for the wise man will not be remembered any longer than the fool,
for in days to come everybody will already be forgotten –
and how the wise man dies with the fool!'

[17] And so I hated life,
for dreadful upon me seemed all deeds that are done under the sun,
for it is all a mirage and chasing after wind.
[18] And I hated all my achievements
for which I had worked so hard under the sun,
for I have to leave them to a man who will come after me:
[19] who knows whether he will be wise or foolish,
and [yet] he will control all my achievements
for which I have worked with so much effort and wisdom under the sun.
This also is a mirage.
[20] So I turned to let my heart fall into despair over all the achievements
for which I had worked so hard under the sun,
[21] for it happens that a man – who has worked hard with wisdom,
       knowledge and skill – must give it – his share! – to someone else
       who has not worked hard for it!
This also is a mirage and a great evil!
[22] For what will a man have for all his hard work
and for the striving of his heart,
that he was such a hard worker under the sun?
[23] For all his life was an excruciating task full of resentment;

even at night his heart could not rest.
This also, it is a mirage!

²⁴ There is nothing good in a human being who eats and drinks
and makes his throat see good in his hard work!
This also I saw: that [the ability to do] this comes from the hand of God.
²⁵ For who can eat and who can enjoy more than me/*without him*?
²⁶ For to the man who is good before him,
he gives wisdom and knowledge and joy,
but to the sinner he gives [the] business to amass and to accumulate,
[only] to give [it] to the one who is good before God.
This too is a mirage and chasing after wind!

³:¹ For everything there is a season;
a time there is for every matter under heaven.
² There is a time to give birth, but there is also a time to die;
there is a time to plant, but there is also a time to uproot what has been
          planted.
³ There may be a time for killing, but there is also a time for healing;
there may be a time for demolishing, but there is also a time for building.
⁴ There may be a time for weeping, but there is also a time for laughing;
there may be a time for lament, but there is also a time for dancing.
⁵ There is a time for throwing stones, but there is also a time for gathering
          stones;
there is a time for embracing, but there is also a time to be far from
          embracing.
⁶ There is a time for seeking, and there is a time for letting go;
there is a time for keeping something, and there is a time for throwing
          something away.
⁷ There may be a time for tearing, but there is also a time for mending;
there may be a time for remaining silent, but there is also a time to speak
          out.
⁸ There is a time for loving, but there is also a time for hating;
there may be a time for battle, but there is also a time for peace.

⁹ What success have the workers from all their hard work?

¹⁰ I saw the task God gave humans to tackle.

[11] Everything he has made beautiful in its time –
he also has put eternity into their hearts –
only that no human can find out what God has done from beginning
    to end.
[12] I knew that there is no good in them,
except to seek happiness and to do good in their lives,
[13] and [I] also [knew] that any human being who can eat and drink and
    see good in his hard work – that is a gift from God.
[14] I knew that everything that God does will remain for ever;
nothing can be added to it;
nothing can be taken away from it;
and God has done [this]
so that they will fear him.

[15] Whatever is now, it was before;
and that which will be, it has been before;
and God seeks out what is being pursued.

[16] And I saw something else under the sun:
in the place of judgment, there was wickedness;
and in the place of righteousness, there was wickedness.
[17] I said to my heart:
'God will judge the righteous just as he judges the wicked;
for there is a time for every matter – and every deed committed there.'
[18] I said to my heart:
'For the sake of human beings, so that God would show them, and so that
    they see:
"They are animals, they are like them."'
[19] For there is the fate of human beings
and there is the fate of animals,
and there is one fate for them:
as this one dies, so dies that one.
And there is one spirit for everything,
and so there is no successfulness for human beings over the animals,
for everything is a mirage.
[20] Everything is going to one place.
Everything came into being from the dust,
and everything is returning to the dust.

[21] Who knows whether the spirit of human beings is going upwards,
and whether the spirit of the animals is going down below the earth?
[22] And so I saw that there is nothing better for humans
than to take delight in all they do,
for this is their share,
for who will bring them to see into what comes after them?

[4:1] Then I turned, and I saw all the instances of exploitation
that are committed under the sun.
And look: the tears of the oppressed,
and they do not have a comforter;
and the hand of their oppressors, strong –
and they do not have a comforter!
[2] And I reckoned luckier the dead, who have already died,
than the living who are still alive,
[3] and better off than both
is the one who has not yet come to be,
who will not see the evil deeds that are done under the sun.
[4] And I saw that all the hard work and all the skill
which are put into the things people do
springs from a man's envy of his neighbour.
This also is a mirage and a chasing after wind.
[5] The fool folds his hands – and eats his own flesh.
[6] Better one full hand with rest
than two full hands with hard work but chasing after wind.

[7] Then I turned, and I saw another mirage under the sun,
[8] the case of a single man without a companion.
He has no son or brother,
and there is no end to all his hard work;
even so, his eyes are not satisfied with [his] wealth,
and [he says]: 'For whom am I working so hard
and depriving myself of the good things of life?'
This also is a mirage, and a dreadful task it is.

[9] Two are better than one
because they have good reward for their hard work.
[10] For if they fall, one can lift up his companion.

But pity the one who is on his own.

When he falls, there is no-one else to lift him up.

¹¹ Furthermore, if two lie down together,

then they can warm each other;

but for the one on his own:

how can he generate warmth?

¹² And while one on his own is easily defeated,

two together can make a stand;

and a three-fold cord cannot be torn quickly.

¹³ Better a child, poor and wise,

than a king, old and a fool, who does not know any more how

        to be warned.

¹⁴ For from prison he had come to be ruler,

even though he had been born poor in his kingdom.

¹⁵ I saw all the living, all who go about under the sun,

with the second child who had come to stand in his place.

¹⁶ There was no end to all the people,

to all before whom he was.

Even so, those who will come after him will not appreciate him,

for this, also, is a mirage and a running after wind.

5:1 [4:17 MT] Watch your feet when you go to the house of God;

and draw near to listen rather than to give sacrifice like the fools do:

for they do not know to do evil.

2 [5:1 etc.] Do not be quick with your mouth,

and do not rush your heart to bring out a matter before God,

for God is in heaven, but you are on earth!

Therefore let your words be few!

³ For a dream comes through many tasks,

and the voice of a fool through many words.

⁴ When you have made a vow to God,

do not delay fulfilling it,

for there is no *pleasure/right time* among the fools.

What you have vowed, fulfil!

⁵ Better you do not take a vow at all

than vow and not keep it!

⁶ Do not let your mouth sin against your body,
and do not say before the messenger: 'It was unintentional!'
Why should God become angry about your voice
and destroy what your hands have accomplished?
⁷ When dreams multiply, and mirages and many words, then
 fear God!

⁸ When you see oppression of the poor
and justice and equity denied in the province,
do not be *frightened/surprised* by the matter,
for one official *watches over/watches out for* the one above him,
and there are more officials above them.
⁹ Yet success from the land, it is meant for everybody;
even the king is served by a field.
¹⁰ He who loves silver will not be filled with silver;
and who loves luxury? No gain!
This also is a mirage.
¹¹ When the good increases, then those who eat it increase.
So what profit is there for him who owns it,
except for the gazing of his eyes?
¹² Sweet is the sleep of the slave,
whether little he eats or much!
But the fullness of the rich permits them no sleep.

¹³ Then there is the case of a particularly sickening evil
that I saw under the sun:
wealth hoarded by its owner to his own misery!
¹⁴ Namely, this wealth was lost in a bad business,
and then he fathered a son, and there is nothing in his hand at all.
¹⁵ Just as he left his mother's womb, naked will he return,
leaving exactly as he had come;
and he cannot take anything for all his hard work,
nothing to carry in his hand.

¹⁶ This also is a sickening evil, just like it:
as he came, so he will leave;
so what success [is there] for him,
that he works so hard for [nothing but] the wind?

[17] Indeed, all his days in darkness he eats,
and resentment increases, and his sickness, and frustration.

[18] See, then, what I have seen as good, which is beautiful:
[for everyone] to eat and to drink and to see the good in all one's
        hard work
which he works for so hard under the sun
during the number of the days of his life which God has given him;
for that is his share.
[19] [I have] also [seen]:
every human being to whom God has given wealth and possessions
and whom he has enabled to eat from it,
and to accept his share and to find enjoyment in his hard work –
it is a gift from God!
[20] For he does not often remember the days of his life,
for God keeps him occupied with the joy of his heart.

[6:1] There is an[other] evil that I have seen under the sun;
and it is manifold on humans:
[2] [the case of] someone to whom God has given wealth and riches
        and honour,
and there is nothing lacking for his throat of all the things that
        he craves;
but God has not given him the sovereignty to eat from it,
because *someone else/a foreigner* devours it.
This is a mirage, a moral disease this is.

[3] If a man fathered a hundred children
and lived many years,
and if the days of his years were many,
but his throat is not filled from this good,
and even [if] a grave there was not for him,
then I would say that a stillborn baby is better off than him!
[4] For in a mirage it comes,
and into darkness it departs,
and in darkness its name is shrouded;
[5] also: the sun it has not seen or known,
and yet it has found rest, more than him.

⁶ And if there were a thousand years twice, but he cannot see
      goodness –
do they not all go to one place?
⁷ All the hard work of the man is for his mouth,
and yet the throat is never filled.

⁸ For what advantage to the wise man over the fool,
and what [. . .] for the poor who know how to advance *in life/against*
      the living?
⁹ Better the seeing of the eyes than the wandering of the throat!
This, too, is a mirage and a chasing after wind!

¹⁰ Whatever has occurred, its name has already been called;
and it is known what that is;
and that the man cannot win a case against one who is stronger
      than him.
¹¹ For it is true: 'the more words, the more elaborate the mirage.'
What advantage for the man?
¹² For who knows what is good for the man,
for the number of the days of the life of his mirage,
which he has made like the shadow . . . which . . .
and who will tell the man what will be after him under the sun?

⁷:¹ Better a name than good oil,
and the day of death than the day of his birth.
² Better to go to a house of mourning
than to go to a house of feasting,
for that is the end of every human being,
and the living should take it to heart.
³ Better resentment than laughter,
for through badness of face the heart becomes good.
⁴ The heart of the wise is in the house of mourning,
but the heart of fools is in the house of joy.
⁵ Better to listen to the rebuke of a wise person
than listening to a song of fools.
⁶ For like the sound of thorns under the pot,
so is the laughter of the fool.
And this also is a mirage!

[7] For the oppression can fool a wise man,

and a gift can destroy a heart.

[8] Better is the end of a *word/matter* than its beginning;

better a long wind than a high wind.

[9] Do not hurry in your spirit to become vexed,

for vexation lodges in the lap of fools.

[10] Do not say, 'How is it that the former days were better than these?'

for it is not out of wisdom that you enquire about this!

[11] A good thing is wisdom with an inheritance,

and an advantage for those who continue to see the sun.

[12] For in the shadow of wisdom, in the shadow of silver;

but the success of knowing this wisdom is this: it keeps its owners alive.

[13] See the work of God:

for who can straighten what he has made crooked?

[14] On a good day, enjoy the good,

and on a bad day, see:

God made that day also, just as he made the other,

on account of the fact that the man cannot find anything that will come
     after him.

[15] I have seen it all in the days of my mirage:

the case of a righteous man who perished in his righteousness,

and the case of a wicked man who prolonged [his life] in his wickedness.

[16] Do not be overly righteous and do not pretend to be excessively wise!

Why harm yourself?

[17] Do not be overly wicked, and don't be a dupe!

Why die when it is not your time?

[18] It is good for you to hold fast to this and also not to let your hand
     go from that.

For the one who fears God will come out of all these.

[19] This wisdom is stronger for the wise man than ten rulers who are
     in the city,

[20] for there is no man *on earth/in the land* so righteous that he does good
     and never sins.

[21] Also, all the things which they say, do not take to heart,

so that you will not hear your slave cursing you!

²² For surely, many times over – your heart knows – you, too, have cursed
      others.

²³ All this I had tested with wisdom.
I had said: 'I want to be wise', but it remained far from me.
²⁴ What happened is far away, and deep-deep.
Who can find it?

²⁵ I had turned, me and my heart,
to know, and to explore, and to search wisdom and competence,
and to understand wickedness, overconfidence and the irrationality,
      stupidity.
²⁶ But I kept finding something more bitter than death: the woman who –
      a tangle of nets she is, and a set of snares is her heart, fetters are her
      hands.
The one who is good before God will be rescued from her,
but the sinner will be captured by her.
²⁷ 'See, this I have found,'
says Lady Qoheleth,
'time after time in searching for competence,
²⁸ which my throat was still seeking, but [which] I have not found:
one man among a thousand I have found,
but a woman among all of them I have not found.
²⁹ See, this alone I have found:
that God made human beings straight;
but they have sought for many schemes.
⁸˸¹ Who is like the wise man, and who knows how to unravel a matter?
A man's wisdom lights up his face,
and the stern expression on his face is softened.'

² – I¹ –
The mouth of the king observe, and because of an oath of God!
³ Do not hurry from his presence when you leave,
do not stand in a bad *matter/word*,

──────────────

   1. The personal pronoun is a 'stage instruction' to indicate that Qoheleth
      is speaking in his normal voice again.

for he can do whatever he likes!
⁴ For the word of a king is supreme,
and who can say to him:
'What are you doing?'

⁵ He who observes a command will not know a bad *word/matter*,
and time and judgment a wise heart knows,
⁶ because for every matter there is the proper time and judgment,
because the evil of human beings is large upon them,
⁷ because they cannot know what will be,
because who can tell them how it will turn out?
⁸ There is no human being who can exert supremacy over the wind,
[no-one] who can restrain the wind,
no-one who can be supreme over the day of death
and no-one who can gain release from military service during the battle;
and neither can wickedness rescue its master.
⁹ All this I saw as I dedicated my heart to all deeds that are done under
    the sun,
a time when the man exerts supremacy over another man to his
    detriment.

¹⁰ And in that same context I saw the wicked being buried.
And they had come,
and they had gone from a holy place,
and they were forgotten in the city where they had acted in this manner.
This really is a mirage!
¹¹ When a sentence is not executed quickly against a crime,
then human hearts are filled within them to do what is wrong;
¹² when a sinner does evil things a hundred times but lives a long life;
because I also know that it will turn out well for those who fear God
when they fear from before him;
¹³ and it will not turn out well for the wicked,
and his days will not lengthen like a shadow,
because he has not walked in fear before God.
¹⁴ It is a mirage that takes place on earth,
the case when the righteous are treated as if they had acted like the wicked,
and the case when wicked people are treated as if they had acted like the
    righteous. This really is, I say, a mirage!

¹⁵ So I recommend joyfulness,
since there is nothing good for the man under the sun,
except to eat and to drink and to be joyful.
For that will go with him through his hard work
during the days of his life
which God has given him under the sun.
¹⁶ When I gave my heart to know wisdom
and to see the business which is done on earth –
even that there is no-one who sees sleep with his eyes by day or by night –
¹⁷ then I saw the full extent of God's doing:
that the man cannot find out all doing that is done under the sun;
however hard he works to search it out, he cannot find it!
And even if the wise person claims to know – he cannot find it!
^{9:1} For all this I gave to my heart in order to examine it all:
how the righteous and the wise and their activities are in the hand of God –
also love, also hatred –
the man does not know anything that is before them.

² Everything is the same for everybody:
one fate for the righteous and for the wicked,
for the good, and for the clean and for the unclean,
for the one who sacrifices and for the one who is not sacrificing;
as for the good, so for the sinner;
the one who swears is like the one who is afraid to swear.
³ This is evil in all that is done under the sun:
that/for there is one fate for all,
and in particular: the heart of human beings is full of evil,
and stupidity is in their hearts throughout their lives,
and afterwards – to the dead!
⁴ Indeed, who [is the one] who should be chosen? – With all the living,
 there is hope.²
As for a living dog: it is better off than a dead lion!
⁵ For the living know that they will die,
but the dead know nothing at all;

---

2. So the *ketib*; the *qere* reads: 'Indeed, who [is the one] who is joined to all
the living? – There is ground for hope.'

and there is no further reward for them,

for the memory of them is forgotten.

⁶ Even their love, even their hatred, even their jealousy have already
     perished;

and they will never again have a share in anything that is done under
     the sun.

⁷ Go, eat your bread with enjoyment,

and drink your wine *with a glad heart/with a good conscience*,

for God has already approved what you do!

⁸ At all times let your clothes be white

and do not let oil be lacking on your head!

⁹ See life with a woman whom you love all the days of the life of your
     mirage

which he has given to you under the sun

during all the days of your mirage,

for that is your share in this life in your hard work

for which you work so hard under the sun!

¹⁰ Everything your hand finds to do,

do with your might,

for there is no work or competence or understanding or knowledge
     or wisdom in Sheol, to which you are going!

¹¹ I turned and saw under the sun:

that the race is not to the swift,

nor the battle to the heroes,

nor bread to the wise,

nor wealth to the insightful,

nor favour to the knowledgeable;

for time and chance happen to them all.

¹² For indeed, human beings do not know their time,

like the fish who are caught in an evil net

and like birds caught in a snare;

like them, so human beings are snared at an evil time,

when it suddenly falls upon them.

¹³ I also saw this [example of] wisdom under the sun,

and it is great to me:

¹⁴ A small city with few men in it,

and a great king came against it, surrounded it and built great siege
      works against it,

¹⁵ and a poor wise man was found in it,

and he was the one who [could have] delivered the city through his
      wisdom,

but nobody paid attention to that poor man.

¹⁶ And I said: wisdom is better than heroism,

but the wisdom of the poor is despised,

and his words are not heard.

¹⁷ The words of the wise in calm are heard,

more than the shouting of a ruler among fools.

¹⁸ Wisdom is better than weapons of war,

but one *sinner/bungler* can destroy much good.

¹⁰:¹ Dead flies cause fine perfume to smell and bubble;

a little folly weighs more than wisdom, more than honour.

² The heart of the wise to his right,

the heart of the fool to his left.

³ And even when the fool walks on the road,

his heart is absent and [*he/it*] tells everyone: he is a fool.

⁴ If the spirit of the ruler rises against you,

do not forsake your position,

for calmness can calm great offences.

⁵ There is the case of an evil that I have seen under the sun,

like an 'inadvertent sin' that comes out from the presence of the
      sovereign.

⁶ Folly has been set up in great heights,

but the rich dwell in the lowliness.

⁷ I have seen slaves on horseback,

while princes are walking on the ground like the slaves.

⁸ He who digs a pit may fall into it;

he who breaks down a wall, a snake may bite him.

⁹ He who quarries stones may be injured by them;

he who splits logs may be endangered by them.

¹⁰ When the iron is blunt and it has lost its edge,

one will whet it and make it sharp and strong again;

and success: wisdom prevails!

[11] If the snake bites because there is no incantation,

then there is no success for the master of the tongue.

[12] The words of a wise man's mouth: favour;

but the lips of a fool swallow him.

[13] To begin with, the words of his mouth are foolish,

but in the end his mouth is evil stupidity –

[14] and a fool multiplies words!

Human beings do not know what is to come,

and what will be after them – who can tell them?

[15] The hard work of the fool, *when will it leave him breathless?*[3]

When he does not know to walk to a city!

[16] Woe to you, O land, when your king is a *boy/servant*,

and your leaders feast in the morning!

[17] Happy are you, O land, when your king is a son *of the freeborn/*
of the noble ones

and your leaders feast at the proper time –

like heroes and not like drunkards!

[18] Because of laziness the roof sinks in,

and because of slack hands the house leaks!

[19] For a laugh they prepare food,

and wine makes life joyful,

and money is the answer for everything!

[20] The king you should not curse, even in your thoughts,

and you should not curse the rich in your bedroom,

for 'a bird from heaven' may carry the sound,

or 'the master of the wings' may tell the matter.

[11:1] Release your bread on to the surface of the water,

for in many days you will find it.

[2] Give your share to seven, or even eight,

for you do not know what evil may happen *on the earth/against the land*.

[3] When clouds are full, they empty rain on the earth;

and whether a tree falls to the south or to the north,

---

3. The translation reflects a slight change in the original Hebrew;
   see discussion in the commentary.

in the place where the tree falls, there it will be.

⁴ Whoever observes the wind will not sow;

and whoever regards the clouds will not reap.

⁵ Just as you do not know how the breath comes to the bones in the
    mother's womb,

so you do not know the work of God, who makes everything.

⁶ In the morning sow your seed,

and until the evening do not let rest your hand,

for you do not know whether this one will succeed,

or whether this one or that one,

or whether these two will be as good as the one!

⁷ And the light is sweet,

and it is good for the eyes to see the sun.

⁸ So, if a man lives many years,

let him rejoice in them all,

and *he will/let him* remember the days of darkness,

that they, too, will be many!

All that is to come is a mirage!

⁹ Rejoice, young man, while you are young,

and let your heart make you good in the days of your youth!

And follow on the paths of your heart and what your eyes see,

but know that over all these things God will bring you into judgment!

¹⁰ And turn vexation away from your heart

and remove evil from your body,

for youth and black hair are a mirage!

¹²ː¹ And remember your *origin/creator/grave* in the days of your youth,

when not yet have come the days of evil

and drawn near the years when you will say,

'I have no *pleasure/part* in them,'

² when not yet will have darkened the sun and the light and the moon
    and the stars,

and the clouds return straight after the rain,

³ on the day when the guards of the house tremble,

and the men of strength are bending themselves,

and the women who grind cease working because they are few,

and they keep dark when they look through the windows;

⁴ when the doors to the street are shut,

when the sound of the grinding has fallen
and one rises up at the sound of a bird,
and all the daughters of song are brought low;
[5] when they are even afraid of what is high and terrors on the road,
the almond tree blossoms,
the locust grows fat
and the caper berry spoils;
because the man is going to his eternal home
and the mourners circle on the street;
[6] when not yet has been plundered the silver cord
and the golden bowl has not yet been shattered
and the pitcher has not yet been crushed against the fountain
and the wheel has not yet been smashed against the cistern,
[7] and not yet has returned the dust to the earth, just as it was,
and the spirit has not yet returned to God who gave it.

[8] 'A mirage, nothing but a mirage,'
says the qoheleth,
'it's all a mirage.'

[9] But there was more to him: Qoheleth was a wise man; he also taught the
          people knowledge; he heard, selected and arranged many proverbs.
[10] Qoheleth sought to find pleasing words, and what is written [here] is
          correct; [these are] words of truth.
[11] Words of the wise are like the goads,
and the masters of collections are like fixed nails,
that are given by one shepherd.
[12] And there is more:
beyond these, my son, be warned! Of making many books there is no end,
and excessive study leads to breathlessness of flesh.

[13] The end of the matter: all has been heard.
God you shall fear, and his commandments you shall keep;
for this is the whole [responsibility] of every human being,
[14] for every deed God will bring into judgment over its hidden motives,
whether good or evil.

COMMENTARY

1. INTRODUCTION TO A PHILOSOPHICAL TREATISE ON HUMAN LIMITATIONS AND HAPPINESS (1:1–3)

Context

The book of Ecclesiastes originated as a speech. The first three chapters, from 1:1 to 3:15, initially look like a philosophical treatise which demonstrates the unsatisfactory nature of human endeavour. From 3:16, a second level of meaning becomes increasingly prominent, covertly encouraging the audience to remain faithful to their religious Jewish traditions in the face of tempting alternatives offered through the occupying power of Ptolemaic Egypt (see Introduction: Date and historical context, and Language and style, genres and intention). Verse 1 is the title of the written record of the speech, introduced as the *words* of Qoheleth. Verse 2 reports his signature statement, that everything is a mirage. It functions as a hypothesis, followed directly by the research question that guides the remainder of the material.

Comment

1. The title identifies the orator as *qōhelet* (*Qoheleth*). The designation is not a real name, but fictitious. It serves as the speaker's nickname (cf. 'Smithy' in English) and its formation as a feminine singular participle indicates that it serves as a professional title, identifying the orator as a professional speaker (cf. 'the smith' = *haqqōhelet*, 'the qoheleth', only in 12:8; see the discussion in the Introduction: Title and authorship). His description as *son of David* and *king in Jerusalem* hints at Solomon, but the fictitious name *Qoheleth* suggests an *anonymous* 'royal' figure. The fact that he was not Solomon would have been obvious to those who attended his performances, but later readers of the book were taken in by the royal aspects of his description. (Indeed, the identification with Solomon persisted into the eighteenth century, and is still held by some.) The pseudonym ensured the speaker's anonymity, in case his manuscript fell into the wrong hands.

2. In the form of an executive summary, Qoheleth's teaching is summed up through his main hypothesis: everything is *hebel, a mirage* (repeated five times).

Many believe that this summary was added to the main part of the book by a frame narrator who created the persona of Qoheleth (Fox 1999: 162). Since the question in verse 3 is a response to this motto, however, it is more likely that the summary is the opening statement of the speech. The phrase *says Qoheleth* indicates that what follows is a record of Qoheleth's *spoken* words.

The word *hebel* is a visual metaphor (see the discussion in the Introduction: Language and style, genres and intention). The metaphor paints the various aspects of life explored in Qoheleth's speech as a mirage, an optical illusion of the mind.

3. The research question asks what may count as true success in life. The question contains three unusual expressions: (1) the word *yitrôn*, 'profit, benefit, return, gain, compensation, satisfaction, success'; (2) the phrase *in all their hard work with which they work so hard*; and (3) the phrase *under the sun*. All three are important for understanding the whole speech.

Qoheleth uses the phrase *under the sun* in two different ways (see the discussion in the Introduction: Language and style, genres and intention). First, it refers to the 'world-as-is', the 'universality of human existence' (Seow 1997: 104), which includes hard work, disappointment, injustice and death as a consequence of the fall (Gen. 3:14–19). Second, it is a cypher for foreign rule over Judea from

Ptolemaic Egypt. The word *sun* is a metonymy for Egypt. As Egypt's most prominent deity it represents the whole country. It also refers metonymically to the Ptolemaic king, for his throne names included the epithet 'son of the Sun'. Through most of the first three chapters (1:1 – 3:15) this second meaning remains hidden, for later readers at least. It becomes more prominent from 3:16–22 onwards.

The verb *'āmal*, 'to work hard', and the corresponding noun *'āmāl*, 'hard work', refer to human exertion and effort in general. Neutral in meaning, they sometimes take on negative connotations relating to troublesome, disappointing work from the context.

The word *yitrôn* is a buzzword trending in Qoheleth's time (see the discussion in the Introduction: Language and style, genres and intention). It epitomized the aspirations of those who wanted to adopt the cultural values of Ptolemaic Greece – economic and social success in the pursuit of personal happiness. In Qoheleth's time, many believed that this was possible as a natural reward for hard work, *without* need for God.

In a world tainted by sin and in a situation where his country remains under foreign rule as a consequence of God's judgment, Qoheleth demonstrates through a series of thought experiments, case studies and reflections that the *success* which many of his compatriots seek through their own effort alone is out of reach. All his attempts end in failure (see comments on 2:11, 13; 3:9; 5:9, 16 [MT 5:8, 15]; 7:12; 10:10–11), demonstrating that this *success* is *hebel*, a mirage.[1]

Given the thesis statement in the previous verse, many believe that the question is rhetorical (Krüger 2004: 47–55). Nonetheless, Qoheleth's speech continues to explore serious attempts to find success. All of them lead to the same conclusion: that all human efforts to find success are doomed. The goals that humans pursue to find happiness are mirages, optical illusions of the mind. Qoheleth's claim is not based on gut feelings, generalizations and

---

1. The term does not appear in the final chapters of the book (Eccl.
11 – 12), presumably because by then Qoheleth considered his refutation of such aspirations to be complete.

anecdotes, but on empirical evidence based on experiments and careful reflections on scenarios which represent the gamut of human experience.

Meaning
Qoheleth's search for success plays itself out *under the sun*, in a fallen, sinful world, as numerous allusions to Genesis 3 later in the book demonstrate. Just below the surface, however, Qoheleth also raises questions about political and cultural independence, and in particular about religious freedom and social justice under foreign occupation.

2. COMPLEXITY OF THE SEARCH FOR HAPPINESS DEMONSTRATED THROUGH POETIC MEDITATIONS ON THE CYCLICAL NATURE OF NATURAL PHENOMENA AND THE LIMITS OF HUMAN EXPERIENCE (1:4–11)

Context

The introduction is followed by poetry, a 'poetically stylized prelude' (Krüger 2004: 48). An elevated form of language, it raises the register of the spoken text. It also lifts the intensity of intellectual, emotional and motivational engagement of the audience. A hidden subtext below the surface of meaning implies that the Greek culture of Ptolemaic rulers from Egypt is not as novel as it may appear to Qoheleth's contemporaries. Opening with a thematic statement (v. 4), it has two parts: descriptions of the earth's constancy (vv. 5–7) and of human transience (vv. 9–11).

Comment

4. Reflecting on the contrast between the constancy of the earth and human transience fosters the intellectual stance which the speaker wants his audience to adopt. The contemplation of nature illumines the human condition. The word *'ōlām* ('for ever, eternal, everlasting') is an important keyword. Regularly associated with God (e.g. 3:14), it contrasts with the limited time span of humans.

The natural cycles explored here are considered permanent and continuous, but also ever changing and dynamic, with the translation *ever the same* aiming to reflect the dynamic beauty of nature's regularity – the 'laws of nature'.

5. The movements of the sun demonstrate the earth's constancy. The verb is *šo'ep*, usually rendered 'hurries' (NRSV, NIV) in English. It is consistently associated with heavy breathing due to physical exertion (Koehler, Baumgartner and Stamm 2001: 1375). The sun either rushes back joyously to its starting point, or it hastily toils across the sky (cf. Ps. 19:6; Longman 1998: 69). The reference to the swift subterranean motion of the sun may simply reflect the physical reality that on most days of the year the period between sunrise and sunset is longer than twelve hours, which would have suggested that the sun moves more quickly during the period when it is invisible. It seems implausible that Qoheleth would have lamented the predictability of solar motion. The sun changing its course and speed or remaining stationary would have been catastrophic. The sun's predictable circular motion is an illustration of the life-sustaining quality of the world's constancy.

6. A description of wind movements further illustrates the world's constancy. The expression *the wind* comes late and last in the verse. This creates a sense of 'pull' through the syntactic vacuum that in itself mimics the movement of air. A succession of recurring and predictable sound patterns through assonance (repeated vowel sounds), alliteration (repeated consonants), anaphora (repetition of sounds at the beginning) and rhyme (repetition of sounds at the end) mimic recurring and predictable wind patterns. The verse mentions three geographic locations: north, south and *its surroundings*. The last term elsewhere describes the location that surrounds a particular entity, the physical vicinity of stationary objects. Reference to the 'local vicinity' of winds must be metaphorical; consequently, it refers to the 'localities-through-time' into which the wind moves through a region along predictable corridors or wind channels. The movement of wind is described in spectacular fashion, with a sequence of seven verbs of motion in swift succession.

This wind moves in recurring patterns through predictable locations. As the poetic artistry of the verse aims to display, it is also beautiful. The verse describes a series of different regional wind patterns with associated weather patterns. Constant in their variety, they appear at regular and thus predictable intervals, year after year. They enable agricultural management, planning for safe and comfortable travel and taking precautions against discomfort or danger. They are 'irregular' when compared to one another, but 'constant' because they are recurring at predictable intervals from one year or season to the next. They are evidence of the earth's constancy. Humans cannot control them, but they can adapt to them. They are object lessons which support a didactic aim throughout the speech – recommendations for coping with adverse circumstances and for taking advantage of God-given opportunities beyond human control.

7. The regular motion of water serves as another illustration of the world's constancy. Describing the one-directional flow of water as the eye perceives it, Qoheleth prompts his audience to contemplate the providential balance of nature – that nonetheless the sea does not fill up and flood, threatening human life. The ambiguity is purposeful, drawing his audience into the progress of his reflection.

8. Generally this verse is taken to express frustration (Murphy 1992: 8; Longman 1998: 71; Krüger 2004: 51). Yet the verse expresses wonder (Provan 2001: 55) and intellectual curiosity. The adjective *yĕgeʿim* is ambiguous. It appears only here and in Deuteronomy 25:18 and 2 Samuel 17:2. The nouns in the other two occurrences qualify human beings who are breathless, physically exhausted from exertion. The adjective is either a metaphor ('physically exhausted') which personifies abstract events or an intransitive verbal adjective which expresses their impact on humans as 'mentally exhausting'. Traditional interpretations result in translations like 'all things are wearisome' (NRSV, NIV). More likely, however, is a positive understanding of 'mental exhaustion'. All these mentally exhausting phenomena are beyond human comprehension. The phrases in 8b and 8c have the same grammar as verse 8a, and this suggests that the phrase *kol-haddĕbārim* (*all these things*) from 8a is elliptic and needs to be supplied mentally by the reader (Longman 1998: 71–72). It is all these breathtaking phenomena that humans cannot adequately describe, that the eye cannot see enough of and the ear cannot hear enough about.

9. Traditionally, interpreters take the next three verses as further reflections on the world (Longman 1998: 72) or as extrapolations that extend the experience of repetition in the natural realm to a corresponding pattern of repetition in the realm of human activities (Murphy 1992: 8; Krüger 2004: 52). In human existence *under the sun*, Qoheleth's cypher for foreign rule, humans cannot achieve anything that is genuinely new. While humans partake in the cycles of nature that repeatedly achieve one and the same thing (Weeks 2012), this only *appears* to reflect human permanence. Verse 10 demonstrates that the limited perspective of humans *misleads* them to think that they can break the cycle.

10. The counterclaim to an apparently new event is perhaps also a veiled allusion to the new circumstances under the Ptolemaic regime, which appears to promise novelty. It is dismissed with the assertion that what appears to be new has in reality been done before, in a past beyond the reach of human memory.

11. The meditation ends with an expanded assertion about the limited purview of human memory (Krüger 2004: 52). However, the expressions that refer to the objects that are to be remembered are ambiguous: do they refer to people, events, or both? The word for *memory* is *zikrôn*, very similar in sound to the *yitrôn* (*success*) which Qoheleth and his audience seek. Verses 4–11 do not aim to provide an answer to the research question of verse 3. Rather, they 'set the scene' for the case studies, reflections and lessons of the rest of the book. Nonetheless, the soundplay links research question and poetic reflection, and this suggests that *yitrôn* (*success*) is difficult to find for those who lack *zikrôn* (*memory*). Below the surface, Qoheleth exposes as old hat the promise of true happiness which Greek culture appears to offer. Its appearance of novelty arises from ignorance of the past.

Meaning
Qoheleth's message in his beautiful, poetical reflection sets up the constancy of the earth as a contrast to human transience in order to foster the intellectual stance which the book's author wants his readers to adopt. It also provides the imaginative and subversive backdrop for the rest of the book by elevating the beauty and stability of creation and forcing the audience to acknowledge

their ignorance about the world at large and the place of humans in it.

As humans marvel with wonder, awe and curiosity at the beauty and permanence of nature, they also come face-to-face with their own limitations. True epistemological innovation is beyond them. Apparent epistemological progress is exposed as an illusion with reference to the limited scope of human memory.

3. CASE STUDY 1, A THOUGHT EXPERIMENT: QOHELETH'S ADOPTION OF THE IDENTITY OF A SOLOMONIC CARICATURE TO EXPLORE HUMAN SUCCESS THROUGH THE UNLIMITED SATISFACTION OF HUMAN DESIRES (1:12 – 2:26)

In his first case study, Qoheleth conducts a thought experiment in which he adopts – for the sake of the argument – the persona of the great king Solomon, who was famous for his wisdom and wealth early in life and for his conspicuous consumption and apostasy later in life (1 Kgs 1 – 11). He explores whether *yitrôn* (*success*) can be obtained through the unlimited satisfaction of human desires. King Solomon may have served as the 'ideal' whom Qoheleth's young audience were striving to emulate in their search for success, perhaps justifying their own accommodating tendencies with reference to Solomon's openness to foreign influence. If even their role model could not find success, however, what chance was there for anyone else? The report has six parts.

A. The preamble to the experiment (1:12–18)

Context
These verses form the preamble to Qoheleth's first case study. It sets out the parameters of the experiment. It also provides a transition

from the preceding poetic reflection to the experiment (2:1–26), and links it to the thesis statement and research question (1:2–3). Qoheleth establishes his suitability for conducting the experiment. He states whom he emulates in his experiment, namely the legendary King Solomon. This clarifies that he has unlimited human resources at his disposal, which makes him ideally suited to conduct the experiment. He emphasizes his approach to the experiment, which is characterized by intellectual rigour. He sets out the object under investigation: every human activity on earth. And he provides an 'executive summary' of the findings obtained in his experiment.

Comment

12. There is only one historic person who fits the description of both *son of David* and king over all Israel: King Solomon. The speaker does not identify himself directly as Solomon, which he could have done with the substitution of one word, *šĕlōmō* (= Solomon), for *qōhelet*. Qoheleth was not the real Solomon, but only took on the legendary king's persona for the sake of his experiment. This signals that he conducted it with recourse to unlimited human resources and practical opportunities, having everything for its successful completion at his disposal. Qoheleth's implicit argument is: if I can show that even someone like the legendary King Solomon could not obtain true success, no-one can. This he proceeds to do in the report on his thought experiment in 1:13 – 2:26. He alerts his audience that they should not take everything he is about to say too seriously. Qoheleth's self-portrayal as Solomon is humorous, exposing the futility of the human search for success.

13a–b. Qoheleth explains the next two parameters of his experiment and provides the first part of an executive summary that explains the reason for the depressing nature of his findings. His approach as lead investigator is characterized by intellectual rigour, by applying his cognitive faculty (*my heart*) to a methodical (*on investigating*) and comprehensive (*and exploring*) examination through skill and know-how (*by wisdom*).[1]

---

1. Throughout the Old Testament, the human heart is roughly equivalent to the modern term 'mind' (see Schroer and Stäubli 2001: 43).

The next parameter concerns the research sample that is the object under investigation: all human and divine activities (*everything that is done*) on earth (*under the heavens*, 13b). The expression refers to human (2:1–24a) and divine activities (2:24b–26). Later, the expression *under the sun* also refers to Judea under foreign rule. Here, Qoheleth uses the alternative phrase *under the heavens* for the sake of plausible deniability.

13c. Stated in the most emphatic terms to introduce the first case study, Qoheleth's executive summary is only the first of a string of similar results to follow. The demanding nature of human endeavours (*it is a dreadful task . . . to tackle*) is God-given, highlighting the theological origin of the human predicament. Qoheleth is not 'deeply perplexed, confused, perhaps even teetering on the brink of total scepticism' (Enns 2011: 39). Rather, Qoheleth's statements about God's interactions with the world function against the background of God's judgment on humans in Genesis 3:16–19.

14–15. The phrase *I considered . . . – and look* is the first of many expressions in which Qoheleth reports the results of his extensive research project. The awkward phrase *every doing that is done* in combination with the cypher *under the sun* signals that more is at stake than human activities in general.

He surveyed *every doing that is done under the sun*. Qoheleth's audience would have caught the political referent of the cypher, but for later readers the phrase appears to denote human existence in general. Its second, hidden meaning as a cypher for Jewish life under foreign rule will only become visible later, from 3:16 onwards. Every *doing that is done under the sun* is (1) a *mirage* (*hakkōl hebel*); (2) a pursuit of the unobtainable, expressed in the beautifully haunting, metaphorically evocative catchphrase *and a chasing after wind*; (3) irreversibly bent (*what is bent cannot be straightened*); and (4) unproductive (*and what is missing cannot be counted*).

16. Qoheleth's claim that he became wiser than anyone who had been king over Jerusalem before him at first sight looks like the somewhat exaggerated self-praise typical of many ancient royal inscriptions (Koh 2006). In reality, it is ironical. He is meant to sound ridiculous: (1) he speaks to himself (*with my heart*), telling himself something that he presumably already knows; (2) the introduction to the quotation is overly verbose: the personal pronoun in the phrase *I spoke, I* . . . is not emphatic but rather highlights the obsessive self-focus with which Qoheleth speaks; (3) the same is true for the next occurrence of the pronoun in 16b–c: *I, look, I have expanded*; (4) the two verbs in 16c, literally *I have expanded and I have added*, are *overly* emphatic and expose the speaker's excessive self-aggrandisement; (5) the expression *more . . . than all who have been before me over Jerusalem* appears silly because there was only one king over Israel in Jerusalem before Solomon, namely his father David; (6) the formulation of the over-the-top claim as direct speech – Qoheleth's Solomonic persona quoting himself! – draws further attention to the self-parody.

17. Qoheleth describes the outcome of his attempts to explore the difference between wisdom and folly (cf. 2:12; 7:25; 9:3; 10:13). The attempt to 'understand' wisdom on the one hand and folly on the other is not a quest for two different things, but a genuine attempt to discover how to make wise decisions in the face of alternatives (contra Enns 2011: 41). The syntactic design of the verse emphasizes a contrast. The two phrases in 17b–c describe what Qoheleth had set out to find. These are expressed with identical infinitive construct forms of the verb 'to know, understand' followed by direct objects referring to intellectual qualities. By contrast, the next phrase presents similar syntactic elements in reverse order, again with the verb 'to know', but appearing now as a finite verb form with the meaning 'to discover'. This chiastic arrangement introduces a contrast and expresses both surprise and frustration over the result. The noun *siklût*, here translated *incongruity* (cf. discussion of 2:3), is extremely rare.[2] Explaining the surprising and frustrating result of his discovery, he expresses this quest as a pointlessly futile endeavour, *a chasing after wind*.

18. Apart from the opening word *for*, the verse reads like a proverb. Shockingly, it claims the very opposite of what is usually claimed for wisdom (cf. 7:16). Qoheleth may have coined it for its counter-intuitive and shocking effect (but cf. 2:13). The emotional

---

2. It occurs only here and, with the alternative spelling *siklût*, in 2:3, 13; 7:25; 10:1, 13.

impact of his discovery is irritating (*kāʿas*, *resentment*) and painful (*makʾōb*, *pain*). Ironically, Qoheleth's experiment has partially succeeded and he has gained more wisdom, but this added wisdom has resulted in disappointment and frustration. As his report on the experiment will demonstrate, wisdom may bring material *success*, but not necessarily greater happiness and well-being. This incongruity is the cause of his exasperation.

Meaning

In verse 13 Qoheleth identifies God as the source of the problem he encounters on his search for *success*. At this stage, it is deliberately left unexplained why God would have done such a thing. This theological puzzle is a key to understanding the theological intent of the book. It is not just something that Qoheleth suddenly discovered through empirical research. Rather, it is something to which he wants to draw his audience's attention.

Qoheleth's experiment does not fail for lack of trying or lack of resources. He had everything at his disposal, intellectually and materially, and still failed to obtain *success*. Our endeavours should also be measured with regard to how our achievements make us feel. Emotions are important. True 'success' should lead to real happiness.

B. The methodology of the experiment (2:1–3)

Context

This is the second of six parts in Qoheleth's first case study. It showcases Qoheleth's introspective methodology through his narration of three internal dialogues in which he addresses his heart (v. 1), personified laughter (v. 2a–b) and personified pleasure (v. 2c–d). It also describes the focus and objective of his intro-spective approach: he wanted to experience the psychosomatic effects of excessive alcohol consumption in order to determine the long-term value of the unrestrained satisfaction of desire for human well-being.

Comment

1. Qoheleth's methodology is not 'empirical', as is sometimes claimed (contra Fox 1999: 75–78, esp. 76). The evaluation of his findings is *introspective*. He adopts the role of *chief investigator* and addresses his heart, the organ of thought and emotion, as the main *co-investigator* on his quest. In the phrase *let me test you by pleasure* he informs his heart of his intention to observe its reactions to his exposure of it to pleasurable experiences which are about to begin, and charges it to report its own rational and emotional responses to him for further evaluation (*and you, see what is good!*). By observing his heart's reaction to the stimuli of pleasure, he intends to gather evidence for his evaluation of the efficacy of pleasure as a means for humans to obtain success, that is, happiness. In order to create a controlled environment for his experiment, he orders his heart to pay attention to its mental states, and to report its findings directly to him. In this way, he intends to form well-documented beliefs about his mind through direct awareness of it (Schroeder 2009). The direct appeal to his heart, *Come on, then*, is not an invitation to the audience. Rather, the *extremely polite* appeal is humorous.

The phrase *and look, this too was a mirage* constitutes the executive summary of the case study, confirming his initial hypothesis: the pursuit of happiness through the unlimited satisfaction of human desires through pleasure also is a mirage. The poetic exuberance of these words adds a light touch and self-ironical flavour.

2. Qoheleth engages in mini-dialogues with personified laughter (*to laughter I said*) and personified pleasure (*and to pleasure* [*I said*]), who become test subjects in the experiment. The exclamation *mĕhôlāl*, [*You are*] *to be praised!*, functions like the cheering on of contestants to stimulate them to give their best. Like a lab rat, laughter is co-opted for the successful conduct of the experiment under the most favourable conditions possible. Pleasure is goaded into ensuring perfect conditions for the experiment through a question that presents her with the challenge to display what she can achieve when she gives her best to the task: *What can you achieve?* The effect is light-hearted and amusing, and as such these recruitment efforts are part of Qoheleth's parody of the Solomonic persona, aimed to entertain.

3. The Solomonic persona reports how he used his heart to explore the psychosomatic effects of pleasure-seeking through the (excessive) consumption of alcohol: *by stretching my body through wine*. An interjection appears to assure Qoheleth's audience that the level of his alcohol intake was moderate: *all the while my heart guiding* [*me*] *by wisdom*. In the self-ironical context of his experiment, however, we are left with the impression that he is self-ironical here, too. This is confirmed through the next phrase, *by grasping a state of irrationality* (*wĕle'ĕḥōz bĕsiklût*).[3] Qoheleth intentionally drank himself into a stupor. He not only stretched his body; he also intoxicated his mind. The final phrases explain the purpose of his excessive behaviour: to appraise the effects of his unrestrained behaviour on his own well-being (*until I would see*) in order to gather evidence for evaluating the long-term effects ([*for*] *the number of days of their lives*) of self-indulgence on human well-being in general (*whether or not this is good for human beings to do*).

Meaning

This passage prioritizes emotional well-being over pleasure-seeking, and as such presents a formidable challenge to one of the most basic tenets of capitalism: that growing consumption more or less automatically leads to more happiness. It also presents a challenge to the church, in the West and in the Global South, which is being influenced by Western values at increasing speed. The challenge is this: if consumption is not a sure way to happiness, what are the alternatives that the Christian faith can offer believers in order to live happy and fulfilled lives (John 10:10)?

C. The report on the experiment (2:4–10)

Context

In deliberately self-absorbed fashion, Qoheleth describes the successful completion of the Solomonic persona's experiment. He reports achievements in the pursuit of happiness through self-indulgence. He emphasizes that the level of his achievements was unmatched, and concludes that his experiment was successful inasmuch as he obtained every material object he had desired and

---

3. The word *siklût* is the same as in 1:17, with variant spelling. The contexts in Ecclesiastes (1:17; 2:3, 13; 7:25; 10:1, 13) suggest a tension with rationality, hence *incongruity* in 1:17 and *irrationality* here.

he reached the highest social status in his society. The most striking feature of this report on Qoheleth's experiment is the high frequency of first person singular pronouns, indicating obsessive concern with self-gratification.

Comment

4–6. The Solomonic caricature's claim to great achievements introduces a list of these in the remainder of the report. The phrase *I made great my works* can be understood in two ways: (1) I enlarged my works; (2) I increased my possessions. Both are intended through deliberate ambiguity. In the following list (vv. 4b–8), each item or group of items comes with the expression *for myself*. Qoheleth emphasizes the self-obsessed nature of these undertakings. The Solomonic persona aligns himself naturally with the audience Qoheleth wants to reach. The list highlights achievements in the area of architecture and landscaping.

7. The following group of items in the list combines the purchase of livestock and humans. The Solomonic persona treated them as commodities to supply his needs and bolster his ego. His servants, male and female, were financially needy and dependent on him. He *acquired* them, presumably as bond slaves due to excessive debt. The curious note that he eventually had slaves born in his service (lit. *I had sons of a house* = home-born slaves) at once suggests that these slaves stayed with him for life (in contravention of the Law of Jubilee, Lev. 25) and also that the experiment he reports on was a longitudinal study, lasting a lifetime. The juxtaposition of slaves and livestock in the list is meant to portray the low esteem in which the Solomonic persona held others. The crowing about the highest number of stock owned probably relates also to the slaves, and adds to the portrayal of the Solomonic persona as boastful, arrogant and inconsiderate.

8. The list continues with the accumulation of other desirable objects, including precious metals and a group of human beings that, alongside gold and silver, the Solomonic persona considered the most desirable assets of high society: he even trained for himself (lit. *I even made myself*) artists and women. The idea of 'making' oneself humans with specific skills or abilities is either sarcastic, exposing the speaker's presumption and quasi-divine delusions (so Krüger 2004: 65), or it refers to facilitating the training of personnel as singers and members of the harem, or both. The expression *šiddâ wěšiddôt* is unique in the Old Testament. The expression is derived from the word *šad*, *breast* (Longman 1998: 92; Koehler, Baumgartner and Stamm 2001: cf. 1420 with 17). In the Hebrew, the phrase *women with big breasts* simply says 'breast and breasts', a deliberately crude idiom similar to the reference to women's genitalia in Judges 5:30, and quite aptly objectified and labelled as *what pleasures men*.

9. Qoheleth lays claim to political and financial supremacy over his predecessors in Jerusalem, in boastful, hyperbolic language. The two verbs 'I became great and surpassed' are not a hendiadys, as many propose, but the use of two verbs when one would have done is deliberately boastful, hence the translation *I became so much greater and richer*. Qoheleth continues to portray the Solomonic caricature as obnoxious and repulsive. The claim to have surpassed all who had been before him betrays the speaker's need for self-affirmation. The comparison with all kings in Jerusalem before him when in reality there was only one was *meant* to sound ridiculous. *Even so*, claims the Solomonic persona, *my wisdom stood by me!* Personified as a faithful devotee to Super-Solomon, wisdom remained his trusty sidekick, no matter what.

10. The Solomonic caricature concludes his report with the assertion that the point of the experiment, namely the unrestrained and complete satisfaction of his desires, was realized. The experiment was 'successful'. In a litotes (a figure of speech with emphatic force through the denial of the opposite of what is being claimed), he affirms that he had not withheld anything from himself that his eyes had desired. Similarly, he had not denied his heart anything it enjoyed from what he had accumulated through all his hard work, linking back directly to the internal dialogue with his heart in verse 1. The expressions stress that complete satisfaction of desires was indeed achieved. The concluding remark in this report confirms that this unrestrained self-gratification was the reward (*helqî, my share*) for all the investment he had made. At this stage, his audience are led to believe that the outcome of the Solomonic persona's experiment was complete satisfaction and happiness, *success* in a real sense. In reality, Qoheleth is setting them up for a rude awakening.

Meaning

The idea that Solomon was not the actual author of the book of Ecclesiastes may be new to many Jewish and Christian believers. The book of Ecclesiastes does not claim Solomon as its author. Recognizing the ironical function of the Solomonic caricature is crucial for understanding the function of this part of the experiment. All this is humorous, funny. Solomon is often seen as the ideal king. However, as 1 Kings 9 – 11 demonstrates, the latter part of Solomon's life was problematic (cf. Hays 2003, who argues that all of 1 Kgs 3 – 11 problematizes Solomon).

The list of the Solomonic caricature's achievements includes not only material possessions, but also a range of cultural achievements, such as architecture and landscape gardening, as well as music. In the Judeo-Christian tradition and in much humanistic thought, these have rightly been considered to be of intrinsically higher value for human flourishing than material goods. Nonetheless, the fine arts and other cultural achievements in and of themselves cannot lead to true happiness.

D. The analysis of the experiment (2:11–16)

Context

This section analyses the value which his achievements held for the Solomonic persona, as a transition from the report (2:4–10) to his emotional response (2:18–23). First, he reports how he took a close look at his achievements and concluded that they were a mirage, not true success. Second, he reports how he considered the epistemological implications emerging from the contemplation of his mortality. Third, he reports the overall epistemological conclusions he drew from his experiment. The passage is a comical internal dialogue, reminiscent of similar internal dialogues frequently presented by modern stand-up comedians. Despite its serious, even depressing content, it is charged with humour and darkly funny.

Comment

11. The unusual phrase *Then I faced* (*ûpānîtî*) which opens the analysis appears for the first time in Ecclesiastes. It suggests that

Qoheleth's Solomonic persona had reached a turning point. He had accomplished all he had set out to do, and it was now time to face the facts. He had contemplated his grand achievements, *all my deeds which my hands had done*, and the amount of effort he had exerted for them (*and the hard work at which I had worked so hard to do*). Both phrases are unusually long and repetitive, artificially stilted in order to draw attention to the emotional and physical effort that he had invested, exaggerated for comical effect.

Three evaluative comments show that all the Solomonic persona's achievements had been an illusion, a pointless effort, leading to the devastating conclusion that there really was no success to be gained *under the sun*. At this early stage in Qoheleth's routine, it may still have gone unnoticed that this is his cypher for foreign rule in Judea.

12. Also introducing it with *And I faced* (*ûpānîtî*), Qoheleth's Solomonic anti-hero reports how he began to face and contemplate the intellectual and epistemological foundations and outcomes of his experiment. His attempt to *see wisdom and folly and irrationality* refers not to a visual experience; rather, it is doubly metaphorical. As an intellectual rather than visual examination, it contemplates the contribution which these concepts can make to the search for success through the unrestrained gratification of human desires.

In his evaluation, the Solomonic caricature asks about the impact of these three intellectual concepts on the fate of his successor: *What will the man do who comes after the king?* The answer is depressing, and expressive of the arbitrariness and incongruous irrationality of human behaviour, no matter how wise or foolish the successor is deemed to be: he will do *just what they have done before!* The Solomon figure anticipates that his successor will make the same mistakes that he himself had committed. People do not learn from the past (cf. 1:9–11).

13. The Solomonic persona launches into what *initially* appears to be an insight (*And I saw that*) into the positive contribution that wisdom can make to human success. He apparently concedes that wisdom is 'successful' in comparison with arbitrarily incongruous behaviour: *there is a success for wisdom over irrationality*. So 'successful' is wisdom that he compares it to light's success over darkness: *just as light has success over darkness*.

14. Wisdom's superior capacity to bring success is then illustrated by means of a proverb. Its content is satirical and undermines the very point that it supposedly means to illustrate. The statement *the wise has his eyes in his head* is a self-evident truism, implying that such a person will walk securely. The second half of the proverb contrasts this with the statement *but the fool keeps walking in darkness.* These observations are banal and self-evident, and do not really further the cause of bolstering the success that wisdom presumably brings. Stating the obvious, the Solomonic anti-hero concedes that wisdom has the capacity to bring at least some success, especially in comparison with irrational behaviour. Yet he belittles that capacity through the faintness of his praise. This ironical concession is then illustrated with another statement of the obvious. People with eyes can see; people without cannot.

This interpretation is confirmed by the next statement, introduced with the phrase *but I also discovered this,* which draws a stark contrast with the previous, apparently positive evaluation of wisdom. What the Solomonic figure has also discovered is that, ultimately, the wise and the fool will end up in the same place: they will all die in the end. The second insight invalidates the value of the first.

In the following verses, the Solomonic persona launches into the report of a dialogue with the co-investigator in his experiment, his heart. Two statements in direct speech are recorded, each introduced with a synonym for speaking.

15a–c. In the first internal dialogue, the Solomon figure applies to himself the insight that all will die: *To the same destiny as the fool I also am destined.* This launches him into a rhetorical question whose form and content reveal the strength of his emotions as he considers the futility of his life's efforts: *Why then did I behave so excessively wise?* The implied answer to the question is: 'For nothing!' Despite the relative value of wisdom in bringing success, his 'wise' behaviour was in vain.

15d. In the second internal dialogue, the Solomonic persona drives home the point: *This also is a mirage!* The devastating verdict that his life's work had been a chasing after an illusion invalidates any relative success that 'wisdom' might have brought him in the short term. Wisdom's apparent success is exposed as a mirage.

16. This conclusion is supported with statements that home in on the finality of death and its consequences, with ever-increasing pathos and emphasis. Through his passionate interjection, no doubt expressed with a loud voice and emphasis, the audience are meant to hear not just the content of his outcry but also his anguish: *and how the wise man dies with* [= *just like*] *the fool!*

Meaning
Through the confessions of the Solomonic persona, Qoheleth exposes the futility of the pursuit of happiness through consumption. Intriguingly, he does this by emphasizing the brevity of life and the certainty of death, the very insight that has led to the pursuit of happiness through consumption in recent times. And so the problem of what can lead to true happiness comes full circle. One answer to the question 'How can we live our lives in ways that truly satisfy and produce lasting happiness?' will be presented by Qoheleth in the concluding part of the experiment, in verses 24–26.

E. The emotional response to the experiment (2:17–23)

Context
The Solomonic caricature now launches into a highly charged report on his emotional response to the experiment. The pursuit of happiness through the unlimited satisfaction of his desires has ended in hatred of life, hatred of his achievements and despair overall, leading to the conclusion that the view of life which had led him down this path was a mirage. His response, which is bristling with frustration and resentment, is three-fold, each part introduced with reference to an emotion: hatred in verses 17a and 18a, and despair in verse 20a.

Comment
17. In his first emotional response, the Solomon figure declares that, as a consequence of his reflection on the outcomes of his experiment, he *hated life*. The Solomonic persona gives three reasons for his aversion to life: (1) He hated life because the *deeds that are done under the sun* were *dreadful upon me* (17b). All human activity, including his own, weighed heavily upon him. The

evaluation is emotional rather than moral. (2) He also hated life because *it is all a mirage* (17c), with the word *all* referring to all the deeds under the sun (= under foreign rule) and all of life. His discovery that the unrestrained fulfilment of his desires had not brought him the success he had been looking for had led to severe disappointment. The promise of happiness and fulfilment through the unlimited acquisition and consumption of luxuries was misleading. The visualization of such happiness through unlimited consumption had turned out to be an optical illusion of the mind. The strong emotion of disappointment is conditioned by the intensity of his hopes, the strength of his desires and the persuasiveness of the promises that had motivated his hard work in the first place (van Dijk 2009). He hated *his* life to the point that he wanted it to end. (3) He also hated life [*because it is all a*] *chasing after wind*. This hauntingly evocative metaphor should not be reduced to the abstract concept of futility. Pursuing luxuries to obtain happiness was like chasing the wind because in doing so he was chasing the wrong thing.

18. Not surprisingly, in the next sentence the Solomon character declares his *hatred* of his life's achievements. The permanently high levels of physical investment paired with the lifelong emotional dedication to his cause – *for which I had worked so hard under the sun* – condition the intensity of his revulsion. It is his early, persistent love for these things that prompts his present feeling of being spurned and betrayed.

In the following statements, the Solomonic persona explains the reasons for his disenchantment.

First, he resents the fact that his life's achievements must eventually be relinquished. He has no choice but to *leave* his achievements *to a man who will come after me*. The deliberately vague, even awkward phrasing studiously avoids admitting that the person he begrudges leaving his life's achievements to is none other than his own son. The Solomonic persona is purposefully portrayed as disagreeable and odious.

19. Second, he raises doubts over his inheritor's competence. While the following statements are presented as a rationale to explain his hatred of his life's achievements, in reality he is trying to justify his negative sentiments towards his successor. Our anti-hero does not really care whether or not his son will have the capacity to administer the inheritance wisely. His real problem is that he himself will lose control.

The short, pithy phrase *This also is a mirage* may refer to everything that the Solomonic caricature has undertaken, from 1:12 to 2:19 (Longman 1998: 103), but it certainly refers to 2:18–19. Qoheleth here lets his anti-hero demolish another possibility for finding 'success', namely, the opportunity for 'successful' young men eventually to pass on their achievements to their children. People with the obsessive–compulsive mindset of the Solomon character will never find satisfaction in *that*, because letting go of their achievements for the sake of someone else, even their own flesh and blood, is just not their thing.

20. In the report of his third emotional response, also in relation to his life's achievements, the Solomonic anti-hero reaches rock bottom. The phrase *So I turned (wĕsabbôtî)* signals a conscious, deliberate course of action. It suggests that his heart's descent into despair was not a gradual, subconscious development forced upon him by extraneous forces, such as those reported by modern victims of depression. Rather, as the expression 'to cause to despair' signals, our anti-hero actively made himself miserable, desperate through loss of hope and interest (Izard 2009: 116).

21. The Solomon persona presents two reasons for his despair. He depersonalizes his own experience and generalizes the mandatory abrogation of human achievements at life's end. The designation of life's achievements as *ḥelqô, his share*, alludes to the short-lived satisfaction our Solomonic anti-hero had briefly felt when he first reached all he had wanted: not quite *success*, but at least some compensation for his labours. What drives him over the edge is the irony that even the tiny return he had wrenched from all his effort was to be abrogated.

Consequently, he evaluates this forced abrogation not only as a mirage, but also as morally wrong (*and a great evil*). In the value system of the Solomonic persona, death and the impossibility of taking one's life's achievements beyond the grave are the negation of all he held dear.

22–23. The Solomon figure presents two justifications for his moral outrage. First, a long rhetorical question implies that the relinquishing of life's achievements at the point of death amounts to a total loss. Second, he recalls that such a life – his own life! – had been emotionally draining and marred by restlessness: *For all his life was an excruciating task full of resentment; even at night his heart could not rest.* Reaching for happiness through the unrestrained satisfaction of human desires made possible through hard work and superior skill really is, after all, nothing but a mirage.

Meaning

The Solomonic anti-hero's experiment has failed. The promise of happiness and fulfilment through the acquisition and unlimited consumption of luxuries was and remains misleading. The visualization of such happiness through unlimited consumption had turned out to be an optical illusion of the mind, similar to the many advertisements which bombard human senses today.

Having all of these aspirations dashed after he had invested his whole life in their attainment was devastating, leaving him with nothing to live for. The intense disappointment made him more than suicidal: it made him *hate* his life. It is not the pursuit of happiness as such that he identifies as futile, but the *pursuit of luxuries* to obtain it. In doing so, he had been chasing the wrong thing. The question that presents itself with urgency is this: how else can human beings find happiness? One answer to this question is offered in the final part of the experiment.

F. The conclusions from the experiment (2:24–26)

Context

At the end of the experiment, a chastened Solomonic persona draws a theological conclusion that is designed to help Qoheleth's audience align their lives with alternative values and practical strategies for a *truly* successful life.

The conclusion is the first in a series of seven similar, refrain-like assertions often called *carpe diem* statements (see Introduction: Theological and practical message) which appear in slightly altered forms in 3:12–15, 22; 5:18–20 [MT 5:17–19]; 8:15; 9:7–10; 11:9 – 12:1. It includes the claim that the ability to enjoy the good things of life is a divine gift.

Comment

24. In his first conclusion, a wiser Solomon figure concedes that without God, humans cannot succeed. The unusual phrasing is rarely reflected in modern translations. Literally, it reads, *There is nothing good in a human being who eats and drinks and makes his throat see good in his hard work.* The statement is painfully negative and incongruently suggests that a non-sensory body part, the *throat*, should be enabled to receive visual sensory input (*makes his throat see*). The throat (= soul) is the place where the deepest emotional and spiritual aspirations are experienced in the human body (Wolff 1974; Schroer and Stäubli 2001). As such, it is able, as it were, to feel emotions and receive other sensory input. It is in this sense that the throat can 'see'.

The difference between the other *carpe diem* passages (esp. 3:22) and this, the first such statement, can be explained against the background of the Solomonic figure. While the other *carpe diem* statements are spoken by Qoheleth, this statement is uttered by Qoheleth's alter ego. As part of his narcissist portrayal, he has not reached the full insight that Qoheleth plans to instil in his audience through the rest of the book, especially through the actual *carpe diem* passages. What he has understood according to Qoheleth's portrayal is the negative side of the lesson – how success cannot be gained. The statement assumes that humans can succeed in obtaining the bare necessities of life *and* are able to enjoy them, but it then clarifies that this is not due to any merit of their own (cf. also Krüger 2004: 72). As the phrase *This also I saw* signals, the remainder of the verse goes on to show the flipside of this insight: *that [the ability to do] this comes from the hand of God.* In other words, the capacity to experience contentment with the simple provisions of life is a divine gift. Qoheleth's alter ego has learned a valuable lesson.

25. The Solomon figure defends his theological conclusion with a rhetorical question that can be, and has been, understood in two different ways. In the first interpretation, he takes recourse to his own life experience: 'For who can eat and who can enjoy more than me?' The rhetorical question implies the answer 'nobody', and so Qoheleth's Solomonic anti-hero uses the rather persuasive example of his life's journey – from ample resources to abundant and grand achievements to disappointment and unhappiness – to drive home the point that, if *he* could not achieve happiness, then no-one can. Readers through the ages have found the *boldness* of the question unfathomable. Could the speaker really have assumed that he was able to eat and enjoy more than any other human being? The Solomonic character's statement relies on hyperbole and is, of course, backed up with his earlier boasts about his grand achievements. Thus, the *boldness* of the claim reflects the comical hyperbole that has prevailed throughout the entire experiment and is exactly in line with the point of why the experiment was conducted in the first place. In the second interpretation, reflected in several medieval manuscripts and most of the versions, readers have *interpreted* the last Hebrew letter in the question as the Hebrew letter *vav* rather than the Hebrew letter *yod*, as reflected in MT, producing the reading, 'For who can eat and who can enjoy without him?' In this second interpretation, Qoheleth's Solomonic figure makes a theological argument that is, ultimately, also based on his life's experience. Since he himself, with all of his resources and almost limitless achievements, had not been able to enjoy them, then no-one can without God's help. Both meanings are equally possible. The ambiguity results accidentally from the near-identical shape of the two Hebrew letters combined with the two letters producing fascinatingly different and fascinatingly meaningful alternatives. In the original oral performance of the experiment, Qoheleth would have chosen one of the two meanings over the other, as the sound of the two alternatives is different. It is now impossible to know which one he might have preferred.

26. The Solomonic persona now moves on to a second line of argument, which affirms traditional beliefs about retribution. He develops this via a description of the various fates of 'sinners' and 'God-pleasers'. Strictly speaking, the Solomonic figure does not develop his own argument, but simply affirms traditional beliefs: *For to the man who is good before him, [God] gives wisdom and knowledge and joy.* In reality, this is not an argument, but just a reaffirmation of the thought his audience has previously abandoned. Perhaps Qoheleth is parading his original anti-hero as an exemplar who has learned his lesson from the disappointment he had experienced over the things he and his audience had been striving for.

The Solomon figure continues his reaffirmation of traditional beliefs with a converse statement: [*the*] *business to amass and to accumulate* describes exactly what his audience were dreaming about. It strikes at the heart of their search for 'success'. The phrase [*only*] *to give* [*it*] *to the one who is good before God* may be aimed at that part of his audience who are still on what he considers to be the correct side. They are given the prospect of reward for their continued faithfulness to traditional values, a potentially powerful incentive.

Much in this concluding remark hinges on the extent of the reference of the demonstrative pronoun *zé* in the statement *This too is a mirage*. Does it refer to all the material since the last *hebel* statement in verse 23, and so to the entire final section of the Solomonic persona's round-off in verses 24–26 (so Longman 1998: 110)? Or does it refer only to the final remark in verse 26? The ambiguity keeps the audience guessing, but a limited reference to verse 26 is more likely on the basis of the content of the statements in verses 24–26, all of which Qoheleth's Solomonic persona and Qoheleth himself affirm and believe to be true and accurate representations of the way the world works.

In the final sentences of his testimony, Qoheleth lets his anti-hero-come-reformed-character drive home the main point of the entire book: the divine redistribution of the emotional and material goods that his wayward audience were hoping to achieve without God renders their goals a *mirage* and a *chasing after wind*. With this, the Solomonic persona has completed his didactic task, and for the remainder of the book Qoheleth abandons it and resumes his original identity as a public orator.

Meaning
A chastened Solomonic figure draws conclusions from his evaluation of the experiment in terms that will guide everything that follows. Without God, human happiness is impossible. Consequently, he advocates for contentment with the simple provisions of life through a lifestyle that is pleasing to God, who rewards those who please him and punishes those who do not. All of us run the same race, and the prize does not go to the rich, the skilful or the powerful (9:11), but to those to whom God will give the ability to enjoy however little or much they have (2:24–26).

4. CASE STUDY 2: THE SEQUENCE AND DURATION OF DESIRABLE AND UNDESIRABLE TIME PERIODS BEYOND HUMAN CONTROL (3:1–15)

Context

In his second case study, Qoheleth explores a regular feature of human experience, namely that the sequence and duration of desirable and undesirable time periods are beyond human control. This case study builds on the first by approaching from a different angle the question of how human 'success' can be reached. The apparently haphazard sequence and duration of favourable and unfavourable conditions for human flourishing are explored, exposing human limitations and emphasizing divine control. The main interest in this case study lies with the divine reasons and intentions for this design. It consists of a short introductory thesis statement in verse 1, a quasi-poetic list itemizing the evidence for it in verses 2–8, a research question in verse 9, and an analysis that offers an answer to that question in verses 10–15.

Comment

   1. The opening thesis of verse 1 introduces a list in verses 2–8. It includes two enigmatic terms. (1) The rare noun *zĕmān*, variously translated 'season' (NRSV) or simply 'time' (NIV). In a chiastic arrangement, it is parallel with the most common word for 'time', 'et. The paraphrase *season* brings out the aspect of *duration* regarding the time periods mentioned in verses 2–8: *For everything there is a season.* (2) The noun *ḥepeṣ* can have many meanings, ranging from 'joy, delight' to 'wish', to 'precious stones' and 'matter, business' (Koehler, Baumgartner and Stamm 2001: 340). The general, all-encompassing nature of the statement suggests a most generic nuance.

The word appears with the phrase *under heaven* (cf. 2:3), a deliberate variation on the more usual *under the sun.* The formulation maintains sufficient similarity to the more common phrase to sustain the theme while introducing enough variation to maintain interest and active interpretive engagement from the audience. The expression is not as loaded with political symbolism as the phrase *under the sun.* It broadens the statement to be less concerned with the prevailing political conditions under foreign rule and more concerned with the conditions of human life in general. The alternative formulation also creates plausible deniability for later assertions, where the cypher *under the sun* barely conceals the regime-critical import of Qoheleth's statements. Consequently, the phrase *a time there is for every matter under heaven* describes human life as such, not Jewish life under foreign rule as the phrase *under the sun* will do with increasing intensity later on. The totalizing thesis that *everything* and *every matter* has its time suggests that the list that follows is meant to be representative rather than comprehensive.

The following catalogue of human activities, arranged in contrasting pairs, has often been described as a 'beautiful poem' (Longman 1998). However, the sequence is a *list* rather than a poem, and gains its poetic quality only from the pairing of under-determined contrasts, which has evocative and thus poetic qualities.

2. Many modern translations render the Hebrew term *lāledet* (lit. *to give birth*) with a phrase like 'to be born' (e.g. NRSV, NIV). Nothing in the Hebrew warrants this. The verb *yld* with the meaning 'to beget' also occurs with men as subjects, and so the human capacity for procreation in contrast with the finality of life describes not so much the totality of life, but rather the rhythm of life, from the most life-giving human activities to their final demise.

The second pair of contrasts emphasizes the rhythm of intense labour during the planting season followed by rest, then intense labour during harvest season – which in the case of root vegetables includes uprooting followed by rest, and in the case of wheat and barley the intense labour of uprooting and ploughing under, followed by another period of rest – until the time for planting next year's crops returns. The phrase describes the natural rhythm of the agricultural cycle with its periods of intense labour followed by rest, a cycle full of promise and reward.

3. The next pair contrasts 'an intentional act to end a life' (Longman 1998: 115) with a restorative intervention to enhance physical and emotional well-being.[1] The more general verb *hrg* with the meaning 'to kill', which can refer to the legitimate or illegitimate ending of human life, rather than the verb *rṣḥ*, which most commonly refers to the unauthorized taking of a life (Exod. 20:13), also suggests that Qoheleth is not referencing the inevitability of extreme violence or injustice. Rather, the rhythm of killing and healing simply reflects the complex realities of life, which sometimes necessitate or make unavoidable the one, and at other times afford the other.

The phrases '"to break down" and "to build up" can be parts of a comprehensive course of action (say, the building or remodelling of a house), which are meaningfully carried out in succession' (Krüger 2004: 77). The numerous archaeological mounds in the modern Middle East are eloquent testimony to the many levels of destruction and rebuilding that occurred over multiple generations in many of the prime locations for human habitation throughout the Ancient Near East. Ultimately, the pattern of rebuilding symbolizes the triumph of the human spirit and the tenacity of local communities, as they keep rebuilding their homes, time and time again.

4. This pair of contrasts lists physical responses to the contrasting human emotions of sadness on the one hand and happiness or amusement on the other. The first pair represents the

---

1. The verb *rp'* can refer to physical and emotional healing, and even to the restoration of good social relations.

most immediate physiological responses to sadness and happiness: *weeping* and *laughing*. The list does not refer to the causes that underlie these responses.

The second pair relates to culturally conditioned, ritual sets of behaviours, namely *lament* and *dancing*. The four activities in this verse, really reactions or responses to emotions or emotional states, are commonly taken to refer to the actual emotions that cause or accompany them (Longman 1998: 115). Lament is a physiological response to the emotion of extreme sadness, and as such corresponds with the other action, weeping, in this verse. Similarly, dancing corresponds with laughter, again in a more expansively physical way that involves movement of the whole body. Both lament and dance are social activities in which human communities share in commiseration over misfortune or celebration of triumphs and other felicitous circumstances.

5. It is not clear whether or not the two converse activities in the first pair in this verse were ever meant to refer to specific kinds of activities, or whether they were created ad hoc to refer to an open-ended range of human endeavours. The idiomatic expressions, enigmatic as they have been to later readers, may have been well-known among Qoheleth's original audience. Whybray, followed by Longman (1998: 116), related them to agricultural praxis: 'the need to clear away stones from a field in order to make it suitable for agricultural use (cf. Isa. 5:2) and, by contrast, to the deliberate ruining of an enemy's field by throwing stones into it (2 Kg. 3:19, 25)' (Whybray 1989: 71).

Alternatively, they may simply mean just what they say: in order to throw more than one stone in quick succession, one needs to have gathered them first. Qoheleth's point may have been about *process*: in order to be able to do something effectively, one needs to have made the necessary preparations. The underdetermined nature of the expression allows for an extremely wide range of human activities, including the building of terrace walls, houses, grave heaps (Fox 1999: 208), and so-called 'watch towers' in vineyards and perhaps other fields (see Isa. 5:2, with specific reference to clearing the field of stones). Alternatively, Midrash Rabbah reads: 'A time to cast stone – when your wife is clean (menstrually), and a time to gather stones in – when your wife is unclean' (Longman 1998: 116; Gordis 1968: 230; Loader 1986: 36–37). Later commentators, medieval and modern, like the idea and interpret these enigmatic expressions as veiled references to sexual intercourse (Fox 1999: 207; see also the paraphrase to this effect in GNB). Not even this can be ruled out, and that is the point.

The expressions *there is a time for embracing, but there is also a time to be far from embracing* are about physical human intimacy, which can include sexual intimacy and other types of friendly exchange (Fox 1999: 208). The verb *ḥbq* refers to a gesture involving close contact of at least the upper bodies of two persons in order to express affection. The entire body may be involved when the occasion includes sexual intercourse (Prov. 5:20). Other occasions may include greetings, welcomes, or the expression of sympathy and comfort (Longman 1998: 116). Alternatively, these statements may simply evoke the human need for discernment: *when* is the right time to do this or that, and how would humans know what the right choice is?

6. All four verbs in this verse lack direct objects, leading to a deliberate vagueness as to what may be sought, let go of, kept or sent away. The statements highlight that appropriate time periods for any of these activities exist, with reference to any number of things. Any specific referents Qoheleth's original audience and subsequent readers may supply are not necessarily identical between the first and the second pairs of verbs. This leads to a bewildering multiplicity of choices on any number of things that a given member of Qoheleth's audience may have wanted to acquire, recover, neglect, abandon, get rid of, keep, guard or protect, reject, share with others, use for investment, and so on. What is the best course of action in the bewildering multiplicity of the complexities of life? These statements evoke the need for discernment in the treatment of material possessions in the complexity of life and highlight how difficult it is for human beings to know the right course of action at any given time.

7. In the first pair of complementary contrasts, the verbs lack direct objects, and various kinds of things may be torn, from clothes to ropes, to more abstract entities like communal ties and international and personal relations. Midrash Rabbah supplies a specific object, clothes, and relates the expressions to mourning

(Gordis 1968: 230–231). In doing so, it responds to the invitation to engage in imaginative interpretation that was created by a gap in the text, but it is a mistake to look for the one correct interpretation. Equally likely and intended are interpretations where *tearing* and *mending* refer to any number of processes related to everyday domestic life (Lev. 10:6; Job 2:12) or even economic and political life. The idea of an appropriate time for keeping silent and for speaking is a regular topic in so-called wisdom literature. The list of complementary pursuits implies that the ability to discern the right timing for the various kinds of activities listed is crucial for human flourishing.

8. The first pair of opposites are emotions, while the second pair refer to large-scale human activities that are commonly fuelled by those emotions. There are times which are more or less appropriate for both of the two emotions and both of the activities, whether they are related or not. There is a time for someone to love another person, for numerous reasons. Chief among these would be a time of crisis, such as a natural catastrophe that creates severe hardship that can be alleviated only through creative acts of love. There is a time for someone to hate somebody else, especially soon after that other person has in some way grievously harmed his or her victim (rape, domestic abuse, cruel exploitation, violent racism, sexual abuse of children, human trafficking, slave labour, etc.).[2] There is a time for violent engagement on a larger scale when one group of humans forcefully and violently threatens the well-being or even existence of another group of human beings (e.g. genocide prevention, self defence). There is a time for peace when an enemy has been defeated or the reasons for war have been resolved, ideally before war breaks out.

9. Almost universally, the question is considered a rhetorical one, with the implied answer: 'None' (Longman 1998: 118). However, this is a genuine question which looks for a real answer. It is prompted by the evidence assembled in Qoheleth's second case

---

2. There will also, hopefully, come a time when he or she will be able to forgive that person, simply in order to be able to move on with the rest of his or her life. But this is not in view here.

study on the sequence and duration of human activities and emotions, and it leads to a thorough analysis and interpretation of that evidence in 3:10–15.

10. With the visual metaphor *I saw*, Qoheleth introduces his observations. He came to realize that the state of affairs attested in the quasi-poetic list – with its complexities, challenges and opportunities – is divinely ordained. It is a task that *God* gave humans to tackle.

11. Here we learn why this state of affairs is so problematic for human beings. God has indeed made everything beautiful and enjoyable, and he has designed humans to aspire to permanent happiness, but the beauty of things does not last, and human beings have no way of knowing how to circumvent the divine make-up of the world. It is this dilemma that leads to such frustration. Verse 11 interprets the fundamental realities that shape human life through the theological perspective of Genesis 1 – 3, in terms of a post-fall creation theology: the world is still beautiful, but human capacity to enjoy it is now seriously debilitated.

12. Qoheleth draws three conclusions: first, that the pursuit of happiness is the only appropriate response to the precarious state of affairs just described (v. 12); second, that human capacity for happiness depends on God (v. 13); and, third, that the divine control over human pursuits is permanent, unchangeable and designed for a purpose (v. 14).

13. Qoheleth affirms his conviction, gained from reflection on his second case study, that *any human being* having the opportunity to *eat and drink and see good in his hard work* is only able to do so thanks to divine providence: it *is a gift from God* (cf. 2:24). *Doing* good makes human beings *feel* good. This is in marked contrast with the first case study in 1:12 – 2:26.

14. The phrase *everything that God does* takes up the beginning of verse 14. The rules by which God continues to order human existence are permanent. However human beings may act, they cannot alter or circumvent the state of affairs that governs the outcomes of their endeavours. The final statement in Qoheleth's third conclusion states the purpose of God's continuing enforcement of conditions after the fall. The religious disposition *fear* [*of God*] which lies behind its verbal paraphrase here is inspired by the idiomatic phrase 'fear of the Lord' so popular throughout the Old Testament (Krüger 2004: 89). The pragmatic function of this statement operates on the level of the book of Ecclesiastes as a whole. The state of affairs pertaining to the divine order of creation after the fall is specifically designed to prompt and sustain fear of God.

15. This concluding reflection makes three more general affirmations. First, the entire state of affairs explored in verses 1–14 is nothing new. Second, Qoheleth helps his audience to view their own perceptions of novelty – prompted perhaps by the new political circumstances of Ptolemaic rule – in the light of eternity.

The final phrase in verse 15 appears opaque to the point of obscurity – *and God seeks out what is being pursued* – and this is reflected in the various interpretations it has received (Fox 1989: 197; Krüger 2004: 90; Longman 1998: 124). A contextually fitting interpretation is to conclude that *nirdāp* refers to that which human beings, Qoheleth's intended audience in particular, are pursuing: happiness. The remainder of the statement then simply affirms, third, that God is concerned for and personally interested in the human quest for happiness.

Meaning
This part of Qoheleth's speech is profoundly theological, but also oriented towards the universal human quest for happiness. Its first part, in the form of a quasi-poetical meditation with staccato-esque sequences of opposite human pursuits and experiences, sets the stage. In answer to the profound question about human purpose in verse 9, the final part of this sequence develops a sustained theological perspective on human life on the basis of the opening chapters of the Jewish and Christian Scriptures, Genesis 1 – 3, and alludes to the limited possibilities for human flourishing after the fall. The divine verdict on humans, especially Genesis 3:17–19, will continue to shape human realities. The state of affairs pertaining to the divine order of creation after the fall is specifically designed to provoke and sustain 'fear of God'. Life is not meant to be easy, precisely in order to remind human beings that they do not have their lives and the outcomes of their endeavours in their own hands.

5. CASE STUDY 3: THE PUBLIC PERVERSION OF JUSTICE (3:16–22)

Context

Qoheleth contemplates the practical consequences from the observation that justice is regularly perverted in the very places where it should be established and maintained. This prompts the first of many reflections on the transience of life and Qoheleth's third piece of advice (after 2:24–26 and 3:12–14) on how to find happiness. Qoheleth's speech begins to turn from the programmatic (1:4–11; 3:1–15) and personal observations (1:12 – 2:26) of the opening chapters to the prevailing sociopolitical and religious circumstances of Jewish life under foreign rule.

After a stylized sketch of the public perversion of justice (v. 16), Qoheleth launches into an extended and highly complex response. Two internal dialogues reaffirm traditional Jewish beliefs in spite of the present circumstances (vv. 17–18) and explore the implications of death for human conduct (vv. 19–21). He then presents a practical conclusion, recommending the active enjoyment of human endeavour (v. 22).

Comment

16. Qoheleth introduces the intellectual exploration of his third case of phenomena *under the sun* which make true success impossible: the public perversion of justice. The word *'ôd* signals that this public perversion of justice is comparable with the two preceding case studies. The near-identical parallelism between the two observations does not make the phrase poetic (contra Longman 1998: 126), but the elevated formulation highlights Qoheleth's moral outrage over the institutionalization of injustice (with Longman 1998: 126).

17. A strong emotional reaction to challenging circumstances again leads Qoheleth to work it through in the form of an internal dialogue.

It is as if Qoheleth initially wanted to reassure himself (and his audience) to resolve the conflict between the ethical ideal and the social reality. The statement is religiously motivated. In support of it, Qoheleth presents a composite argument to himself. First, he takes up an earlier affirmation: *for there is a time for every matter* (cf. 3:1, 11, 14). The next phrase then applies this general truth to the situation at hand. God has ordained that there will be a time for judgment in the future – the vindication of the righteous and the judgment of the wicked on the one hand, and the punishment of the systematic perversion of justice on the other (Krüger 2004: 115). Through the word *there* in verses 16–17, Qoheleth also references the sociocritical cypher *under the sun* in verse 16, mounting a scathing critique of the legal system under foreign rule, not only injustice in general.

18. Qoheleth explains to himself that God's two-fold future judgment (v. 17) has a didactic purpose. His language indicates the importance of what God wants to teach humans. It rhetorically prepares for the sarcastically funny punchline, aimed at the foreign overlords: that *They are animals!* The statement is meant as an insult to those who deem themselves better than others (the foreign overlords), and its shock value (surprise) and provocative reversal of status makes it funny for Qoheleth's indigenous Jewish audience.

19a. The statements about the fate of humans and animals are stilted in their repetitiveness. The slow-burning build-up highlights what follows. Their common fate is death. A first, theological implication arises from the universality of death. Animals and humans have the same life spirit, the spirit of God that will leave them at the point of death (cf. 12:7). This links the experience of death common to humans and animals to divine judgment on wickedness (cf. Gen. 6:3; 6:17). The following phrase states a second, practical implication: *and so there is no successfulness* [*môtar*] *for human beings over the animals*. The word *môtar* is formed from the same Hebrew root (*ytr*) as the buzzword *yitrôn, success* (1:3; 3:9).

19b–21. Next come five reasons in support of this conclusion: (1) everything is a mirage; (2) everything is going to the same place; (3) everything came into being from the dust; (4) everything is returning to the dust; and (5) who knows whether the spirit of human beings is going upwards and whether the spirit of animals is going down below the earth?

Real success for humans in comparison with animals is impossible. This is not a denial of life after death (with Longman 1998: 130). Rather, it is a challenge to the idea, implicit in Qoheleth's rhetorical denial of it, that human beings automatically go upwards upon their deaths, irrespective of their behaviour while alive *under the sun*.

22. Qoheleth now presents his practical response to the public perversion of justice. He affirms the active enjoyment of human endeavour as the best response to the public perversion of justice. In defence of this startling response, he first affirms the active pursuit of happiness as a share, that is, a *partial* success (*ḥeleq,* cf. 2:10, 21), that lies within human reach.

Meaning

Qoheleth begins to address the situation of social injustice under foreign rule. He is outraged over the institutionalization of injustice, enshrined in the legal system under the oppressive foreign rule. His response is theological. Not only will there be divine retribution against the wicked, but also God will somehow vindicate – and thus compensate – the righteous. The theological anchor for Qoheleth's claim is found earlier in the chapter (3:1, 11, 14). In the light of uncertainty about life after death, Qoheleth concludes that *there is nothing better for humans than to take delight in all they do.* The ability to do this, however, is dependent on God.

6. CASE STUDY 4: AN INQUIRY INTO PERVASIVE EXPLOITATION AND SOCIAL INJUSTICE (4:1–6)

Ecclesiastes 4:1–16, after the first main 'theological' section in Ecclesiastes (3:16–22), is deliberately designed to present several case studies of or object lessons from particularly illusory aspects of life, as a counterpoint to the theological passages 3:16–22 and 5:1–7 which frame it. Chapter 4 is another exploration of life *under the sun*, and while chapter 1 was an observation of the cosmos, chapter 2 a self-observation and chapter 3 another cosmos observation, it seems that chapter 4 presents a series of shorter observations of 'mundane' aspects of life.

This chapter and the beginning of the next are composed of four different parts: (1) Case Study 4: an inquiry into pervasive exploitation and social injustice (4:1–6); (2) Case Study 5: on loneliness despite 'success' (4:7–12); (3) a first practical interlude: reflections on the illusory nature of youthful wisdom (4:13–16); and (4) a second practical interlude: instruction on the proper conduct in worship and the keeping of vows (5:1–7).

Context

The fourth case study presents an inquiry into the pervasive nature of social injustice *under the sun*. These realities preclude real success under the oppressive conditions imposed by foreign rule. This is the fourth in a series of five case studies or experiments, all of which are designed to demonstrate the futility of the search for *success* (*yitrôn*). It consists of three parts: his observation of pervasive instances of exploitation (4:1); his emotional responses to this observation (4:2–3); his insights concerning the motivations for human behaviour (4:4–6).

Comment

1. The phrase *Then I turned, and I saw* signals a deliberate shift of focus, towards all the instances of exploitation that are being committed *under the sun*, the cypher for the oppressive foreign regime. Four short expressions report Qoheleth's emotional response to the severity of suffering he observed. They highlight his sympathy for the oppressed and his moral outrage over the fact that social injustice goes unopposed. Qoheleth is not just sorry about this sad state of affairs (Fox 1989: 201; Longman 1998: 131); he is deeply concerned and morally outraged.

2. When Qoheleth exclaims *And I reckoned luckier the dead, who have already died, than the living who are still alive*, he does not present 'death and pleasure as an anesthesia against the hard realities of life', and this is not 'a failure of nerve' (contra Longman 1998: 134). Rather, the overtly redundant form of expression suggests that Qoheleth wants to say more than claim that death is preferable to a life without hope; the overly expansive statement signals a defiant act of political subversion. He praises those generations of fellow Jews who had died before his day – the generations of Judeans who lived before the Babylonian exile – as luckier than the present generation, because they enjoyed national autonomy and relative economic freedom, while Qoheleth's own generation has to subsist under foreign rule and the exploitative system of their alien overlords.

3. The term *'äden, not yet*, supports this interpretation. Qoheleth specifies as better off those who have not yet been born rather than those aborted before birth, those stillborn, or those who never

were and never will be born (Longman 1998: 135). What he really
aims to say is that because of the pervasive injustice in his day, he
reckons that earlier generations, who lived before the present
period under foreign rule, had a happier life (v. 2). He also reckons
that there will be a time in the future when Judea will have regained
its national independence (v. 3). It will be a generation *who will not
see the evil deeds that are done under the sun* (= under foreign rule).

Qoheleth envisages this time as a time of political restoration
and religious autonomy. His dramatic statement is not an expression of resigned fatalism, but a thinly veiled outcry over the
injustice imposed by foreign rule. When he ironically 'praises' those
who have died over those who are still alive and have to suffer
constant exploitation, this amounts to a radical critique of the
foreign regime.

4. Qoheleth shares an insight (*And I saw*) which he gained from
his fourth case study: that the motivating factor for human effort
and skill is envy. His appraisal of this circumstance could not be
clearer: as envy compels people to keep up with the material
advance of their neighbours, their effort and ingenuity are
delusional and futile.

5–6. Qoheleth addresses a counterclaim to the conclusion at
which he has just arrived, by means of two proverbs which cancel
each other out. The first proverb fits into a series of sayings that
ridicule sloth in order to promote industry: *The fool folds his hands –
and eats his own flesh*. Qoheleth takes up this proverb as representative
of the arguments that the people he disagrees with might use to
justify their pursuit of success at any cost. In response, Qoheleth
counters their proverbial argument with another proverb, one that
supports his own values: *Better one full hand with rest than two full hands
with hard work but chasing after wind*. This latter proverb trumps the
first because it promotes modesty, balance and contentment over
the pursuit of excess material goods.

Meaning
Qoheleth is deeply concerned over social injustice. Oppression is
a pervasive human experience, in general and in situations where a
people group is ruled by a foreign power (*under the sun*). He also
draws attention to the depth of suffering which the oppressed have

to endure (*tears*). He emphasizes the callousness and brutality of the oppressors (*the hand of their oppressors, strong*). He stresses the shocking circumstance that no-one seems to care (*and they do not have a comforter*, twice!). And he exposes envy as the motivating factor for human misconduct.

7. CASE STUDY 5: ON LONELINESS DESPITE 'SUCCESS' (4:7–12)

Context

In this fifth case study of a series of five in which Qoheleth aims to demonstrate the futility of the search for success, Qoheleth now turns to the case of a person who, having achieved material success, remains unhappy due to his or her social isolation. Its special contribution to Qoheleth's overall argument is the demonstration that human success is measured not only in material goods, but also in the quality of people's social life.

Comment

7. The phrase *Then I turned, and I saw*, identical with the beginning of 4:1 which introduced the preceding case study, again signals that Qoheleth shifts his focus to investigate a new topic, here identified in advance as *another mirage under the sun*. It concerns one of those promising projections of happiness through material success that the foreign overlords had been dangling in front of the eager eyes of Jewish youngsters.

8. The kind of person under consideration here seems to have been a well-known phenomenon in Qoheleth's time: much wealth, but a sparsity of meaningful relationships. No matter how much wealth this solitary individual amasses, it is never enough to make him happy or satisfy his desire for more.

This is confirmed by means of an internal dialogue. The rhetorical question *For whom am I working so hard and depriving myself of the good things of life?* implies its answer. There is no-one whom this person's strenuous labour and self-denial – which presumably accelerate the accumulation of wealth – will benefit, at least no-one whom he cares about.

The next phrase completes the description of the case study with Qoheleth's own evaluation: *This also is a mirage, and a dreadful task it is.* An evaluation where something was declared a *dreadful task* already appeared in 1:13, where the Solomonic persona had pointed out that it was God who had appointed such a dreadful task to humans. Here, by contrast, a more specific task is under consideration, and the blame is not put on God; the emblematic solitary individual himself is at fault. What follows are practical conclusions from his case study.

9. The opening phrase mimics so-called 'better' sayings in the book of Proverbs, asserting the superiority of companionship over solitude: *Two are better than one.* The following phrase provides the first reason for this claim, in general terms: *because they have good reward for their hard work.* This is then further explained through three mini scenarios.

10. The first of these relates to 'crisis management'. When people who live in community or work in a team *fall* – a metaphor for any given crisis – they can help one another up; that is, they can overcome the challenges they face more easily through mutual support. By contrast, the person who has to face such challenges on his or her own is unfortunate and helpless.

11. The second mini scenario functions literally and metaphorically. It describes what happens when people have to spend the night in cold weather conditions. Those who have a companion can keep each other warm. Not so the solitary individual.

12. Terse language pervades the third mini scenario. One person is easily overpowered; the brevity of this phrase makes the Hebrew awkward, but it just about makes sense. The positive impact of companionship in adversity is expressed with the next phrase: *two together can make a stand* (lit. 'the two will stand over against him [= the assailant]'). This and the entire section is capped with a supporting proverb: *and a three-fold cord cannot be torn quickly.* The proverb draws on the authority of traditional wisdom to drive home the point that has been made all along: that life in community is far superior in every way to a solitary existence. There is no place for individualism and self-reliance in the thought-world of Qoheleth.

Meaning

The importance of community over material wealth is one of Qoheleth's core values for human flourishing.

The mention of a *three-fold cord* has prompted Trinitarian interpretations from Christian readers. While a Trinitarian perspective lies beyond Qoheleth's intended meaning, it is either a happy coincidence or, more likely, the result of divine providence that Qoheleth used the number three in his illustration of the strength of human community relations. Combined with the apparently *unmotivated* use of the number, this created an *invitation* to later Christian readers to detect Trinitarian symbolism.

8. FIRST PRACTICAL INTERLUDE: REFLECTIONS ON THE ILLUSORY NATURE OF YOUTHFUL WISDOM (4:13–16)

Context

The eighth unit, 4:13–16, forms the book's first practical interlude, containing reflections on the illusory nature of youthful wisdom in government. It is generally assumed that this anecdote is a theoretical reflection on the limits of wisdom. However, the descriptions of the rulers form a miniature case study with sufficiently precise details to arouse suspicion that Qoheleth was commenting on actual rulers known at the time, despite the vagueness of his language. Consequently, this interlude is in reality a reflection on the corrupting influence of power, similar to the modern adage 'Power corrupts; absolute power corrupts absolutely.'

Comment

13. A traditional 'better' saying affirms the advantage of youthful corrigibility over powerful incorrigibility in old age, with special reference to royal government. Its proverbial form creates ambiguity, leading to uncertainty over a range of interpretive issues (Krüger 2004: 103).

This ambiguity is deliberate. These four verses together may warn against becoming overly enthusiastic about a recently appointed or soon to be appointed new ruler. The consciously ponderous formulation in verse 15 of the reference to *all the living who go about under the sun*, employing the by now familiar cypher for foreign rule in a knowingly awkward phrase, aims to draw attention to this for those in the know. Ambiguity ensures plausible deniability. For later readers, however, this ambiguity creates the impression that this practical interlude forms a more general reflection on what can reasonably be expected from rulers: even the best of them become corrupted in the end.

Despite its vagueness, the description is detailed and specific enough to suggest that Qoheleth may have had real-life events in mind. The main emphasis lies on the *loss* of intellectual virtue in the old king. The phrase suggests that at one time, when he was younger, the king *had* known how to be warned, a capacity that enabled him to become king in the first place but is now lost to him. Qoheleth's reflection has universal and timeless relevance. Even when able governance can be expected from new rulers on the basis of their early track record, they eventually tend to succumb to the corrupting influence of their own success, ending up old, foolish and unwilling to learn. Those who follow their leadership and put their trust in them follow a mirage. They run after the wind.

14. Two observations defend the claim that the ability to learn in a young and poor person trumps the power of a king in old age, if that king has become incorrigible. First, Qoheleth notes how a new ruler rose from prison to royal status, despite his birth in poverty. Only the intellectual virtue of teachability could have made this possible, and this conclusion is suggested by the causal particle *for*. Qoheleth seems to be deliberately vague about the identity of the successful new ruler. Is he referring to the early phase of the king of verse 13b, at a stage when he was still willing to learn, or is he referring to the poor and wise child of verse 13a? Either way, Qoheleth's main point remains unaffected, and this is probably the point.

15. In his second observation, Qoheleth highlights the popularity of *the second child*. The definite article indicates that this second child is known to Qoheleth's audience. For readers of Qoheleth's speech in the book of Ecclesiastes, this means that *the second child* must refer to the poor and wise child of verse 13. It has been proposed that the expression refers to a third individual (Longman 1998; Whybray 1989; Crenshaw 1987; Fox 1989). However, the introduction of a third king cannot account for the definite article in the phrase *the second child*. Furthermore, the assumption that such a short passage treats no fewer than *three* different individuals seems far-fetched. Finally, the idea that three successive kings have risen from rags to riches to replace one another outside the hereditary system of succession also seems far-fetched. In sum, it seems best to remain with the more traditional interpretation that the passage refers to two individuals, both of whom initially rose to royal dignity through wisdom. The expression *the second child* of verse 15 refers to the *poor and wise* child of verse 13. He is called the *second* child because verse 14, which narrates the rise from rags to riches of the old king of verse 13, implicitly treated him as the *first* child, the original rags-to-riches child prodigy.

Qoheleth observes (*I saw*) how the new ruler, who had replaced the now old and unteachable king on the throne of his kingdom, initially enjoyed unlimited popularity not only among all of his own subjects, but with *all the living, all who go about under the sun*. Apparently, his popularity was not just nationwide, but universal (Longman 1998). Nonetheless, the cypher *under the sun* signals that Qoheleth is talking about the oppressive foreign rule in Judea. Yet the statement is not just an exaggeration; the length of the phrase and its over-the-top formulation suggest more. Sarcastic in tone, the global claim apparently being made serves a wider rhetorical purpose in line with Qoheleth's overall aims. His reflection concerns not just any ruler, but the most powerful man on earth, a sovereign ruler who has achieved ultimate popularity.

16. Qoheleth's object lesson concerns someone of whom he could say *There was no end to all the people, to all before whom he was* (note the repeated *all*). The phrases suggest that this king was someone whom all humans alive at the time willingly acclaimed and obeyed. For this man, youthful corrigibility has yielded the ultimate reward: global domination! The excessive claims being made serve as a rhetorical escape hatch, to create plausible deniability. For in reality,

Qoheleth is talking about the foreign ruler over Judea, who ruled with an iron fist and seemed all-powerful and invincible to everybody under his control. Yet all of this comes crashing down in the three short statements that conclude Qoheleth's reflection.

Qoheleth denies the existence of a long-term advantage in the acquisition of power through wisdom, introduced with the expression *gam*, *Even so*, to draw an emphatic contrast. Even with all of this king's present power and acclaim, *those who will come after him will not appreciate him*. The negated verb describes the emotional disregard of later generations for this 'supreme ruler', despite his present importance.

Qoheleth states this prediction as a matter of fact, presumably because its accuracy is readily apparent. In Qoheleth's eyes, fame and power do not outlast the people who possess it. In the final two phrases, he rationalizes this absence of commemorative veneration against the background of two observations that have formed the basis of his teaching throughout: *for this, also*, he observes, *is a mirage and a running after wind*. The referent of the demonstrative pronoun is not just the lack of appropriate appreciation in verse 16, but the entire object lesson gained from his analytical reflection on the opening proverb's veracity.

Ultimately, however, Qoheleth is still commenting on political circumstances of his day. His remarks targeted the hopes for a new and better foreign ruler which many among the Jewish population entertained at the time. The purpose of his anecdote is to promote political realism. Expectations that a foreign ruler might herald a golden age are illusory. Falling for such promises is a chasing after the wind. Ultimately, the new ruler would be found to be no better than those who had gone before him, and that is why appreciation for him would fade.

Meaning

As already noted, Qoheleth's reflection is universally and timelessly relevant. Over time, human leaders tend to lose their ability to learn in reverse proportion to the growth of their success and power. Not only do they eventually tend to succumb to the corrupting influence of their own success, but all too often they naturally attract self-serving sycophants who shield them from critique, even their own. Such bootlickers are naturally drawn towards those with power and success. And those who already surround them tend to adapt their behaviour in that direction, in order to please the all-powerful boss and avoid reprisals for provoking his displeasure. Finally, the more the ruler's sense of absolute power grows, the more he will want to surround himself with those who pander to his delusions of omnipotence. The final claims in this part of Qoheleth's speech are daringly and shockingly subversive. He maintains that those who fall under the spell of such unrestrained autocrats follow a mirage and run after the wind.

9. SECOND PRACTICAL INTERLUDE: INSTRUCTION ON THE PROPER CONDUCT IN WORSHIP AND THE KEEPING OF VOWS (5:1–7)

Context

In the Hebrew versification, the first verse of chapter 5 is counted as the last verse (4:17) of chapter 4. Consequently, in the Hebrew, chapter 5 has only 18 verses, and the English verse number 5:2 is counted as 5:1 in Hebrew.

This second practical interlude turns from reflections on exploitation and social injustice as a consequence of flawed governance to an exhortation about proper worship, with particular focus on reverence for God and religious conduct. Qoheleth unfolds a religious programme which calls his audience to a more theocentric attitude: the fear of God, expressed through reverent worship and practical obedience to the traditional demands of Jewish religious praxis (Krüger 2004: 109).

Qoheleth addresses his audience directly for the first time, in a series of instructions. The rhetorical shift, the religious theme and the exhortatory nature of the sequence with its high concentration of instructions (ten verb forms with imperative force in just seven verses) indicate that Qoheleth has come to the theological centre of his message. In the wider context of 3:16 – 5:7, Qoheleth's exhortation about worship offers an alternative religious vision for his Jewish compatriots.

Comment

1. Qoheleth instructs his audience to be mindful *while they are still on their way* to the place of worship (Crenshaw 1987).[1] The instruction concerns not only proper conduct while participating in worship, but also the practical ethical behaviour of worshippers and their spiritual preparation before their participation in public worship. Qoheleth is concerned not only with his audience's conduct in worship, but also with their lifestyles (cf. Ps. 40:6–7; Prov. 21:3; Isa. 1:10–17; 58:1–14; Jer. 7:1–15; Hos. 6:6; Mic. 6:6–8).

Qoheleth also urges his audience to approach God receptively. Through listening to the word of God, recited and explained in public worship, worshippers learn how they should obey God in all of their lives outside the time and place of worship (Bartholomew 2009). The terse formulation of these two instructions belies their profundity.

Qoheleth's third instruction is implied through its opposition to the second: his audience should draw near to listen/obey *rather than to give sacrifice like the fools do*. The assumption behind this instruction is that fools also offer sacrifices, but their behaviour in general exposes their religious conduct as hypocritical (cf. 1 Sam. 15:22; Prov. 15:8a; 21:3, 27; Sirach 34:21–27).

Although the phrase *for they do not know to do evil* is obscure, so much is clear: the sacrifice offered by the fools envisaged here is inconsistent with the genuine purpose of sacrifices (see Prov. 21:27). It is offered although the behaviour of these fools contradicts the moral values and religious sentiments which their sacrifices are meant to reflect (Krüger 2004: 107). Such sacrifice is an attempt 'to appease God and to silence the conscience' (Hengstenberg 1869:

---

1. Since sacrifices are mentioned, it appears that the Second Temple built shortly after the exile is in view, while other worship locations are also implied.

136; quoted in Bartholomew 2009: 204) of those whose deeds outside the temple walls are wicked and unjust.

2–3. Qoheleth urges his audience to be slow to speak when they converse with God. The instruction is not to speak slowly, but to give oneself time to think before beginning to speak. The second directive adds nuance. The phrase *do not rush your heart* suggests a conscious resolve to slow down and think before bringing a matter before God. But why is it necessary to think before bringing a matter before God? A range of answers have been suggested (Krüger 2004; cf. Lohfink 2003; Bartholomew 2009; Fox 2004). In the light of Isaiah 55:8–9, the statement about the respective locations of Qoheleth's audience and their God does not emphasize the spatial separation between God and humans, but the discrepancy between human expectations on the one hand and God's abundant generosity on the other. It is better for worshippers to listen to God's word, to simply present their requests in the sure knowledge that God is already favourably disposed towards their desires; there is no need for extravagant promises in the form of oaths to motivate divine reward. After all, the temple was a location of God's presence, where God would favourably respond to the petitions of worshippers (1 Kgs 8:27–30; see also Matt. 6:7–8). The next verses continue Qoheleth's emphasis on religious matters. Worship is not merely a matter of the heart; it is also a matter of conduct.

4. The first instruction on the fulfilment of vows emphasizes that the pledges promised on such occasions should be honoured on time. This verse speaks into a common practice. When people made public vows in the temple, the Levites recorded the value of what had been pledged (Lev. 27:14–15). The record would often have included the due date when the worshipper was required to fulfil the vow and hand over the pledge to the temple. This would either be upon receipt of divine blessings in exchange for the pledge, or upon a due date fixed when the pledge was made.

The remainder of the verse provides a justification for this instruction: *for there is no pleasure/right time among the fools.* As so often in Ecclesiastes, we encounter an entire phrase that has several meanings, created through the ambiguous impersonal construction *there is no* and the multivalent term *ḥepeṣ*, 'pleasure' or 'proper time':

(1) *ḥepeṣ* means 'pleasure' and the impersonal construction refers to people in general: 'for there is no pleasure in fools'. The statement in and of itself is true under most circumstances. However, it is also stating the obvious and does not contribute much in the present context; (2) *ḥepeṣ* means 'pleasure' and the impersonal construction refers to God: 'for he [God] has no pleasure in fools'. This fits the context better, and it is certainly true; (3) *ḥepeṣ* means 'the right time' and the impersonal construction refers to the kinds of fools who think defaulting on one's pledge before God is a good idea: 'for there is never the right time [to honour one's pledge] for fools'. There are always people who will find a justification for refusing to make true on their promises, and such people, Ecclesiastes asserts, are fools. All three interpretations are intended here. The phrase is ironical, caustically sarcastic: people who think that they can get away with hypocrisy are nothing but fools. Like Qoheleth's original audience, we are meant to get the joke and laugh at their naïveté. The following verses confirm this verdict, for they demonstrate that the God who dislikes such behaviour will hold such airheads to account.

The second instruction on vows (v. 4d) is simple and direct: *What you have vowed, fulfil!* The unusual word order, with the direct object placed before the imperative, calls attention to the obligation that has arisen from the oath.

5. Three different kinds of statements – a general truth (v. 5), a dual instruction (v. 6a–b) and an extended rhetorical question (v. 6c–d) – function contextually as arguments in support of the preceding charge.

First, Qoheleth claims, *Better you do not take a vow at all than vow and not keep it!* The statement, appended to the command of verse 4 without conjunction for dramatic effect, asserts a general truth with argumentative force: a vow disavowed is not a trifling matter; it will draw dire consequences. In doing so, it functions just like a proverb in an oral performance context.

6. Second, Qoheleth urges, *Do not let your mouth sin against your body.* This first prohibition needs to be understood in the light of its twin: *and do not say before the messenger: 'It was unintentional!'* Qoheleth condemns one of the excuses commonly made to justify non-observance of vows made, namely the declaration that defaulting on a vow was *šĕgāgâ*, an unintentional sin or 'mistake', in line with Leviticus 4:2–35; Numbers 15:22–31; and Deuteronomy 23:22–24. The first injunction anticipates the content of the second. The excuse which the vow-breaker plans to offer in order to justify the disregard of his obligation will prove offensive to God (see below) and incur practical consequences in the real world. The verse envisages what seems to have been a common practice among some (the kinds of people whom Qoheleth calls *fools*), namely to delay paying their due on time, in the hope that the temple personnel would either forget about the pledge or simply not bother enforcing its payment. This delay tactic further explains the directive of verse 4, where Qoheleth has already urged vow-makers to pay their pledges on time. Qoheleth anticipates that the vow-breaker's lame excuse will be exposed for what it is: an attempt to defraud God. This naturally leads to Qoheleth's next argument.

Third, Qoheleth asks, *Why should God become angry about your voice and destroy what your hands have accomplished?* The question takes for granted that news of a vow-breaker's failed ruse will invariably reach God and draw his wrath and judgment. The curious reference to the vow-breaker's voice is in line with the overall theme of speaking in Ecclesiastes 5:1–7. It envisages that the vow-maker has indeed achieved his goal, a divine bequest of material success on the work of his hands in exchange for his pledge. Yet now, in response to the vow-maker's defaulting on his pledge, God will take it all away again.

7. Since the syntax is unusual, this verse has received a variety of interpretations (Murphy 1992: 51; Longman 1998: 155). Qoheleth enumerates things – dreams, mirages and many words – that increase numerically. The idea that *many words* should increase appears oddly redundant, but the phrase refers to verbosity, and so the point of the enumeration is that three kinds of negative activities multiply: the pursuit of unrealistic aspirations (many *dreams*), the pursuit of mirages (*hăbālîm*) and the pursuit of loquaciousness (*many words*). In the context of a sustained tutorial on proper conduct in public worship, the mention of mirages creates a powerful play on words. On the one hand, *mirages* refers to the wildly ambitious – and thus unrealistic – aspirations of Qoheleth's target audience, the young men in a hurry to get rich. On the other hand, there is an allusion to *idols* as mirages. Qoheleth sarcastically suggests that his target audience have allowed their pursuit of economic success at the expense of the traditional values of their Jewish religious heritage to turn into *idolatry*. In an environment when such damaging behavioural patterns proliferate – particularly in public worship but also in social interactions generally – Qoheleth urges his listeners to resist such trends and hold on to God in reverent obedience: *then fear God!*

Meaning

Throughout the Old Testament, entering sacred space demanded special preparation and spiritual conduct (Exod. 3:5; 19:10–11, 14–15; 19:17, 20–24). Where the Christian tradition has identified sacred spaces or 'thin places', Christians have often visited these locations as part of an extended pilgrimage, accompanied by intentional and often intense religious practices like extended prayer and fasting, including an emphasis on repentance and personal holiness.

Sometimes in the Christian tradition, these practices have become so externalized that they lack sincerity. The Reformation in the sixteenth century was, in part at least, a reaction against abusive practices in the church at that time. By the twenty-first century, however, the pendulum among Protestants has swung in the opposite direction and to the other extreme.

Personal and intimate access to God is often taken for granted, and this can sometimes be observed in the casual informality of much modern worship in Western churches, particularly among Protestants. Such informality is intended to reflect intimacy with God, aiming to reflect the casualness of close family relationships and the relaxed attitude among best friends. However, it can also sometimes lead to a kind of familiarity that subconsciously breeds contempt, misleading well-meaning Christians into forgetting that, while God is indeed their Father and Friend, he is also the Creator and King of the universe. He gave himself to suffer on the cross for our sins. He is never to be taken for granted. Modern Christians and churches would do well to hear again the words of Qoheleth: *Watch your feet when you go to the house of God.*

10. THIRD PRACTICAL INTERLUDE: INSTRUCTION ON THE PROPER RESPONSE TO SOCIAL, ECONOMIC AND LEGAL INJUSTICE (5:8–12)

Context

Qoheleth explores practical responses to social, economic and legal injustice. This practical interlude resembles the traditional Instructions or Lectures in Proverbs 1 – 9, which combine information with practical advice.

Comment

8. Qoheleth focuses on the experience of institutionalized injustice *in the province* (*bammĕdinâ*). Longman proposes a negative interpretation: 'While the previous passage [5:1–6] simply urged caution before divine authority, the present one urges *resignation* before human authority' (Longman 1998: 156–157). However, the passage is calculatedly ambiguous in order to create plausible deniability.

The designation *mĕdinâ* – a semi-technical term commonly used for administrative districts under Persian and Ptolemaic jurisdiction – suggests that Qoheleth's Judea was under foreign rule. The noun is formed from the Hebrew verb *dyn*, which refers to the enactment of justice. The irony is trenchant. The phrase *oppression of the poor* refers to social injustice. The words *and justice and equity denied* refer to legal injustice. And this comprehensive oppressive system has been institutionalized through the political hierarchy. Even the monarch of the occupying foreign power may be implicated.

When you see all this, Qoheleth impresses on his audience, *do not be frightened/surprised by the matter.* The verb *tmh* has two main connotations: 'to be surprised' and 'to fear' (Koehler, Baumgartner and Stamm 2001: 1744; Murphy 1992: 51). Multivalence continues with the next phrase, which motivates the instruction. Here the verb *šmr* also has two main connotations: 'to watch over' and 'to watch out for/protect'. This enables two possible interpretations all at once, hearing either a compliant or a non-compliant statement of the entire instruction with its motivation: (1) 'do not be *frightened*, for one official *watches over* another!' In this compliant interpretation, Qoheleth would be reassuring his audience that all will be well in the end, due to the checks and balances of the bureaucratic system; (2) 'do not be *surprised*, for one official *watches out for* another!' In this non-compliant interpretation, Qoheleth would be exposing the institutionally corrupt nature of the state hierarchy, and he would be persuading his audience to expect nothing less than corruption from representatives of the occupying power.

Qoheleth wants representatives of the foreign regime to hear the compliant version of his instruction. He wants his target audience to hear the defiant version, for he does not want to leave them dejected. He helps them realize that such exploitation is only to be expected from a hierarchy sponsored by foreign rule. He does not urge resignation; rather, he promotes realism and fosters resilience.

9. The two-line statement reads, literally: 'And the success of the earth, for all it is; a king for a field served' (*wĕyitrôn 'ereṣ bakkōl hi' melek lĕśādê neʿĕbād*).[1] It is relatively easy to identify the meanings of the individual words in this short pronouncement, yet it is underdetermined. The overall effect is confusing (Eaton 1983: 101; Krüger 2004: 113). This extreme multivalence is deliberate. It is the mention of the king – in close proximity to an only slightly veiled

---

1. The *qere* reading has *hu'* instead of the *ketib* reading *hi'*.

critique of institutional corruption – that prompts this hyper-ambiguity, for the closer Qoheleth's pronouncements get to the seat of power, the more dangerous his situation becomes.

Qoheleth speaks in a mode of communication that is also exploited by modern stand-up comedians, where social critique is regularly expressed through innuendo and humour, the real meaning emerges from the speaker's intonation and body language, and so on. In the live performance of Qoheleth's speech, the subversive intent of his reference to the king would have been obvious to most, but if called to account later, Qoheleth could plausibly deny any subversive intent, as the conflicting modern interpretations demonstrate:

> This verse seems to see an advantage in the existence of the king – and
> thus the top of the hierarchy of the highly and more highly placed –
> and therefore to express an antirevolutionary, sceptical conservatism
> (Kroeber), which still holds the monarchy to be relatively better than
> anarchy (Zimmerli).
> (Krüger 2004: 115)

Modern and pre-modern interpreters fell for Qoheleth's concealment tactics because they missed the irony behind the text's ambiguity. Krüger is one of the few who has noted the statement's hidden regime-critical potential: 'v. 8 [v. 9] – understood as a statement about the advantage of the monarchy – can hardly be read other than as an ironic "quotation" of "official" Ptolemaic power ideology' (Krüger 2004: 119).

10. A short but intense reflection on money and conspicuous consumption follows. It is designed to promote self-restraint and moderation in the pursuit of happiness through material goods. Qoheleth uses a traditional proverb or one shaped by himself for the occasion in order to reflect on the disappointing effects which the love of money and the desire for conspicuous consumption have on the emotional states of human beings. Qoheleth claims that those who love money will never have enough money to be satisfied. He also claims that those who indulge in conspicuous consumption will similarly be disappointed. The assertion is phrased memorably: *and who loves luxury? No gain!* Obsession with

opulence invariably ends in frustration. The unusual construction of the phrase suggests its origin in oral performance, where a high pitch, pause and emphasis gave the presentation a humorous tinge to amuse the audience by setting them up (in the question) for disappointment (in the laconic answer). In conclusion, Qoheleth exposes the pursuit of happiness through greed and indulgence as illusory: *This also is a mirage.*

11. Qoheleth now explains why the love of money and the pursuit of happiness through conspicuous consumption are illusory. Growing wealth naturally leads to a proportionate growth in consumption. This thwarts any hope for surplus, a conclusion expressed through a rhetorical question (*So what profit is there for him who owns it . . . ?*) with an inbuilt partial answer (*except for the gazing of his eyes?*). This unusually constructed rhetorical question implies the answer: 'Nothing, except for the gazing of the eyes.' The phrase is underdetermined, but most likely expresses a yearning, wistful gazing at the goods one has obtained. The scene is pathetic and comical.

12. Likely neither a traditional proverb nor one shaped by Qoheleth for the occasion, this is a saying born out of adversity, perhaps coined by Qoheleth's Jewish community in sarcastic resistance to the repressive foreign regime. *Sweet is the sleep of the slave, whether little he eats or much!* The second half of the proverb exposes the fate of the rich oppressor: *but the fullness of the rich permits them no sleep.* The noun *śāba'*, fullness, can refer to three different things: material surfeit, a full stomach and emotional satisfaction. The resistance proverb exploits this capacity to create a sarcastic play on words designed to mock the foreign exploiter and to amuse the home crowd. The exploiters' material surfeit leads to a bad conscience and consigns them to regrets and self-doubt. Their conspicuous wealth leaves them to feel exposed to the resentful envy of others (see Tamez 2000: 82). Guilt and fear keep them awake, and their overeating causes them indigestion. Their intestinal discomfort keeps them running all night.

Meaning
Qoheleth is a socially engaged poet who challenges corrupt government from the perspective of those who suffer the consequences

of injustice. His veiled, funny, yet scathing critique complements the prophetic literature from the perspective of ordinary people's experience, and does so with a refreshing sense of humour.

11. CASE STUDY 6: ON SELF-INDUCED MISERY THROUGH THE HOARDING OF WEALTH (5:13–15)

Case Studies 6, 7, 8 and 9 combine into a series with profound insights on wealth and misery. The four case studies naturally fall into two pairs. The concluding reflection on all four case studies (6:10–12) is included with that for the second pair.

Context

Qoheleth explores an emotionally catastrophic event, a particularly sickening misfortune. The scenario, whether hypothetical or an actual event, is paradigmatic. It concerns an instance of wealth hoarded by its owner to his own misery.

Case Studies 6 and 7 belong to a series of scenarios which demonstrate that the pursuit of happiness through the accumulation of material wealth invariably ends in bitter disappointment. These and the following two case studies and their conclusion provide a powerful motivation for the exhortation on religious matters in 5:1–7, where Qoheleth had presented an alternative, religious vision for his audience.

Comment

13. Through the rhetorical instrument of real-life scenarios, Qoheleth demonstrates that the pursuit of happiness through material affluence is futile. The introduction marks Case Study 6 as a particularly disturbing case.

It is not clear whether what Qoheleth has observed as a consequence of foreign rule in Judea (*I saw under the sun*) was the story of a particular family he knew, or whether his case is hypothetical. Its description is sufficiently generic yet realistic to be representative of a wide range of human experience, then and now. It concerns an instance of *wealth hoarded by its owner to his own misery*. He declares it to be an emotionally catastrophic and devastating event.

14. What follows is a description of why this case of hoarding wealth has had such a detrimental emotional effect. First, this hoarded fortune was eventually lost. Second, although the hoarder had a son who might have inherited his fortune, he now had nothing to pass on to his offspring. The verse appears to make two separate points: (1) material wealth may be lost randomly, at any time; (2) having been in possession of a fortune without enjoying its benefits, either for oneself or for one's children, makes its loss all the more frustrating. In sum, stockpiling material goods for their own sake is pointless.

15. Most interpreters assume that this next statement provides further grounds for the emotional devastation caused through the loss of the father's fortune, although they do not make a case for this assumption. Longman's comment, in turn, is strangely incongruous: '[The father] was the one who labored so hard in vain to amass wealth. Now death spoils it' (Longman 1998: 166). This does not make sense. How can death spoil the hard-earned fortune, when it is already gone?

Alternatively, it may be the *loss* of the hoard that causes the painful reflection. However, this also does not make sense. Even if the father still had the hoard, and even if he had been able to pass it on to the son, and even if much of it were still left at their point of death, it is obvious that neither of them could have taken any of it with them, under any circumstances. That is just what death does. It is not as if Qoheleth was the first Jew who had ever noticed this.

Therefore, the statement *Just as he left his mother's womb, naked will he return, leaving exactly as he had come; and he cannot take anything for all his hard work, nothing to carry in his hand* is an independent further reason why the act of hoarding wealth for its own sake is in itself a reason for misery.

This can be demonstrated through a comparison with Psalm 49, a victimized poet's reflection on death as an equalizer between himself and his affluent, more powerful enemies (49:6–7). The verses that follow form an extended reflection on universal mortality, focusing on the futility of his opponents' material resources in the face of death (49:8–15), as opposed to his own fate: 'But God will ransom my soul from the power of Sheol, for he will receive me' (49:15 NRSV). This leads into a wisdom instruction (49:16–20) addressed to 'all inhabitants of the world, both low and high, rich and poor together' (49:1–2 NRSV). Here is an excerpt:

> Do not be afraid when some become rich,
>   when the wealth of their houses increases.
> For when they die they will carry nothing away;
>   their wealth will not go down after them.
> (49:16–17 NRSV)

The thought of postmortem impoverishment, here of one's enemies, is comforting and faith-sustaining.

Through the intertextual allusion, Qoheleth draws on the theological and psychological force of Psalm 49. The axiomatic affirmation of human mortality functions as a theological and anthropological antidote to the depressing habit of people hoarding wealth for its own sake. Since wealth may be lost at any time and for countless reasons (v. 13), and since one cannot take material goods into the grave (v. 14), the pursuit of happiness through the hoarding of wealth can only end in miserable frustration, and this is Qoheleth's point.

Meaning

In 5:18–20, Qoheleth himself draws practical conclusions from Case Studies 6 and 7. For this reason, the *Meaning* of the present material will be presented after the comment on 5:18–20.

12. CASE STUDY 7: ON SELF-INDUCED MISERY VIA THE PURSUIT OF SUCCESS THROUGH HARD WORK (5:16–17)

Context
Qoheleth explores a scenario that is as disturbing as the previous one. The pursuit of happiness through hard work also leads to self-induced misery because no-one can take material belongings with them into the grave.

Comment
16. The introduction marks this as a case that is as disturbing as the previous one (*This also is a sickening evil, just like it*). The apparently redundant phrase *just like it* creates the impression that Qoheleth overstates the similarity between the two cases. This is for comic effect, preparing the audience for his next quip. Verse 16b (*as he came, so he will leave*) – a purposeful variation on verse 15 – focuses the problem on the fact that no-one can take material possessions beyond death.

This prompts a rhetorical question (*so what success [is there] for him . . . ?*) which implies its answer: he will achieve nothing. The idea that no-one can take material belongings beyond death is not a new one for Qoheleth and his Jewish community. Rather, it is a well-known truth that others before Qoheleth had used to good effect in situations of crisis to find comfort and encouragement in their faith. It is, however, a traditional idea on which Israelite and Jewish beliefs disagreed with those of neighbouring cultures. Virtually all surrounding cultures entertained beliefs in the after-life, and Egyptian beliefs were particularly elaborate, such that well-to-do Egyptians traditionally received lavish material pro-visions to take with them into their graves and, it was believed, into an afterlife that was not so different from their lives in the here and now (Hodel-Hoenes 1991). It is against foreign beliefs in an afterlife that Qoheleth here reasserts traditional Jewish thinking. His aim was to counter the idea that material belongings could lead to real success and lasting happiness, an idea that had been gaining credibility among his audience, perhaps against the background of the lavish treasures hoarded in the graves of the wealthy in Ptolemaic Egypt.

The next phrase is the final putdown to this idea, because it characterizes a person who holds such views as someone who *works . . . hard for the wind* (*šeyyaʿămōl lārûaḥ*). This turn of phrase differs significantly from the more common phrase *a chasing after wind* (e.g. 4:6) and its variant *a running after wind* (e.g. 4:16). Those expressions characterize various activities as futile endeavours. The phrase here, by contrast, characterizes someone who pursues happiness through material goods as investing his or her hard work in *wind*! In conjunction with the allusion to indigestion (*ḥaśśābaʿ*) in verse 12, it does not take much effort to work out just what kind of 'wind' Qoheleth is thinking of. Qoheleth employs humour to further his argument. The phrase, it turns out, is not an ethical evaluation or an economic prediction; it is meant as an insult to expose such a person's ambitions as ridiculous.

17. The irony continues and reaches its climax. In drastic hyperbole, Qoheleth makes a serious point in a light-hearted manner by describing in exaggerated fashion, not unlike a modern stand-up comedian, the sheer misery that awaits such a person. *Indeed* (the emphatic particle *gam* is the perfect vehicle to launch his punchline), he says, *all his days in darkness he eats*! The word order highlights the frustration of those who suffer from the results of their own success. Their extreme frugality, prompted by miserly concern for the preservation of their hoarded treasure, leaves them utterly miserable – *and resentment increases, and his sickness, and frustration.*

Meaning

In the following verses (5:18–20), Qoheleth himself draws practical conclusions from Case Studies 6 and 7. For this reason, the *Meaning* of the present material will be presented after the comment on 5:18–20.

13. CONCLUSIONS FROM CASE STUDIES 6 AND 7 (5:18–20)

Context

The material in this section, the first of two interludes in Case Studies 6–9, draws conclusions from Case Studies 6 and 7.

Comment

18. Qoheleth presents conclusions in the form of two fundamental insights. The words *what I have seen as good, which is beautiful* have two functions: to create a contrast with the dark fate of those who pursue happiness through stockpiling material goods, and to signal the importance of what comes next.

The strikingly positive features of this introduction contradict more negative interpretations (e.g. Longman 1998: 168). The two adjectives, *good* and *beautiful*, identify Qoheleth's recommendation *to eat and to drink and to see the good in all one's hard work* as morally desirable, physically beneficial and emotionally rewarding.

The phrase *to see the good in . . . one's hard work* is ambiguous and has two intended meanings. On the one hand, seeing the good in something refers to a recalibration of one's standards for assessment. Hence the recommendation is to adopt a lower, more realistic level of expectations regarding what one's hard work can accomplish, and then to be content, even pleased, with that. On the other hand, seeing the good in something may refer to a more proactive strategy of making the best out of one's opportunities for meaningful work. Hence the recommendation is to do one's work as well as possible and to take pride in that. Both options are equally possible, and both are intended.

The end of the verse describes the origin and purpose of the lifelong process of hard work that is so central to the experience of human life. It is hyper-ambiguous. The phrase *which God has given him* qualifies the preceding phrase – *which he works for so hard under the sun during the number of the days of his life* – but it is not clear whether what God has given to humans is life as such, or the brevity of human life, or the circumstance that one's life contains so much hard work, or the circumstance that all this hard work has to be done *under the sun* – that is, under the constraints of foreign control.

In the final phrase of the verse, Qoheleth declares the human ability to enjoy what he considers good and beautiful to be a divine gift, one's *share* (or 'portion', *ḥelqô*) from God, with the personal pronoun *hû'* functioning as a demonstrative pronoun referring to the three coping mechanisms earlier in the verse. The entire sequence of two rather depressing case studies ends on a decidedly positive note for those who are willing and content to receive as a gift from God what they cannot grasp for themselves: happiness despite the limits imposed on human aspirations *under the sun*.

19. Qoheleth's second insight is an expansive reaffirmation of verse 18, emphasizing several theological claims about human enjoyment of material possessions (cf. 5:13–17) as a *share* from God. The statement includes at least four claims that are central to Qoheleth's theology. (1) Everyone who is able to *secure* wealth can do so only through divine providence (*to whom God has given*). (2) Everyone who is able to *consume* his wealth can do so only through divine providence (*and whom he* [= *God*] *has enabled to eat from it*). (3) Everyone who is able to be contented with a limited allocation of material possessions can do so only through divine providence (*and whom he* [= *God*] *has enabled to . . . accept his share*). (4) Everyone who has these three skills in combination can exercise them only because that aptitude is a gift from God. In sum, Qoheleth here promotes economic modesty and self-restraint regarding the consumption of material goods as pathways to emotional fulfilment dependent on divine generosity.

20. Qoheleth defends these four theological claims with two observations about happy people. First, they rarely engage in nostalgia. Second, God enables them to live in the moment.

Meaning

Qoheleth's conclusions fit into a larger canonical context where God is intimately concerned with human happiness and flourishing. Jesus expresses it best: 'I came that they may have life, and have it abundantly' (John 10:10 NRSV). How this abundant life can be found practically is explored in this part of Qoheleth's speech sequence. It can only be received as a gift from God (cf. Jas 4:2–3). The modern science of happiness relates the experience of happiness to gratitude and altruism rather than to the satisfaction of self-oriented desires (Lyubomirsky and Kurtz 2009: 203).

14. CASE STUDY 8: ON A COMMON CAUSE OF MISERY DESPITE ABUNDANT WEALTH (6:1−2)

Context

Case Study 8 continues to develop the argument that the pursuit of success (= happiness) through material affluence is a mirage.

Comment

1. The introduction marks another case study in misery (lit. *evil*). The relative clause *that I have seen under the sun* again signals that Qoheleth reports a case that he has witnessed under the socio-political conditions of his time. The final phrase in verse 1, *and it is manifold on humans*, implies that Qoheleth's example story is representative of the fate of many, and signals its strongly negative impact on the population's morale.

2. Qoheleth describes this common cause of misery, portraying someone who experiences abundant wealth and popularity as a result of divine providence. This person has received from the deity virtually unlimited material resources to satisfy his needs and desires: *and there is nothing lacking for his throat of all the things that he* *craves*, a turn of phrase which employs traditional Hebrew idiom (*throat*) for human desire and aspirations.

In the next part of the verse, however, Qoheleth comes to the crux of the matter: the divine gift of *consumption* has been withheld: *but God has not given him the sovereignty to eat from it* – continuing the metaphor of food consumption for satisfaction in general – *because someone else [nokrî] devours it*. The tone of this brief note is caustically sociocritical. The metaphor of eating slips from the world of human desires to the cravings of wild, scavenging animals who snatch the carrion from one another, and it is combined with a sarcastic, barely hidden play on words in *nokrî* – the word can mean 'stranger' and 'foreigner' – to sarcastic effect. Again, Qoheleth employs ambiguity to create plausible deniability. The various common interpretations of the verse, some of which are listed by Krüger, demonstrate the effectiveness of Qoheleth's rhetorical concealment tactics, then and now (Krüger 2004: 124 n. 31).

Yes, God is the one who has withheld the opportunity for consumption; but does Qoheleth blame God for this, as Longman proposes (Longman 1998: 170)? A look at texts like Deuteronomy 28:30–33 and Nehemiah 9:36–37 reveals that there are divinely sanctioned consequences for human behaviour for which they themselves are responsible (Krüger 2004: 125). Conditions of exploitation under foreign rule – during the exile and beyond, as they currently exist – are brought about through God's judgment upon his people's consistent unfaithfulness and disobedience over time, and this is Qoheleth's point.

In the final part of verse 2, Qoheleth evaluates the socio-economic and political climate that makes the case under scrutiny here such a common and frustrating experience in his time: *This is a mirage [zê hebel], a moral disease this is [woḥŏli rāʿ hûʾ]!* Those who hope to gain material advantage through collaborating with the foreign powers are pursuing a mirage. They may receive material rewards in the short term, but all of it may be taken away at whim. The second evaluation provides moral commentary on the Jewish collaborators' traitorous behaviour, or on the occupying power's manipulative strategies, or both, declaring them *a moral disease*, a condemnation in the strongest terms.

Meaning

Reference to Deuteronomy 28:30–33 and Nehemiah 9:36–37 reveals the underlying theological cause of the real issues that Qoheleth considers. Conditions of exploitation under foreign rule – during the exile and beyond, as they currently exist – are brought about through God's judgment upon his people's consistent unfaithfulness and disobedience over time. Collaboration with the foreign regime may yield short-term rewards, but it is wrong and it will end in misery.

15. CASE STUDY 9: A SPECIFIC CAUSE OF MISERY DESPITE ABUNDANT WEALTH (6:3–9)

Context

Case Study 9 also continues to develop the argument that the pursuit of success (= happiness) through material affluence is a mirage.

Comment

3. This also is a case study, but it is different from the preceding ones. This is signalled formally through a shift from *yēš* (*There is*, in 6:1 and elsewhere) to the conditional particles *'im* (*If*, v. 3) and *wě'illû* (*And if*, v. 6) as well as through the content, which speaks of super-human virility (v. 3a) and longevity (vv. 3b, 3c, 3e, 6a). The scenario is stunning, exaggerated and unrealistic. The first description refers to superabundant progeny: *If a man fathered a hundred children*. The second description simply refers to a long life, *and lived many years*, but it does not end there: the following phrases stretch the defin-ition of longevity. The next line contains an enigmatic statement, literally 'and many which will be the days of his years'. Its unusual syntactic design signals an equally unusual meaning, *supernatural* longevity.

The next-but-one line reads *and even [if] a grave there was not for him.* There are three possible meanings to this phrase: (1) it may allude to Enoch (Gen. 5:24); (2) it may refer to the lack of a proper burial (Longman 1998: 180); (3) it may be a hyperbolic and hypothetical reference to immortality. The arguments in favour of this third meaning are strong, for it brings this otherwise enigmatic and awkward phrase in line with its context as part of a hypothetical scenario that reflects the wildest dreams of those whom Qoheleth targets in his discourse. Finally, verse 6a states *and if there were a thousand years twice.* This fifth description is explicit in its reference to a supernaturally long life.

The descriptions in verses 3 and 6 portray a hypothetical, supernatural life, a thought experiment: even if someone were to achieve all these things – the abundant wealth and popularity of verse 2 and the abundant progeny and immortality of verses 3 and 6 – the fact that he is not able to enjoy the fruits of his achievement (*but his throat is not filled from this good*) means that all he would have is more mouths to feed without adequate resources, with the ultimate punishment of having to endure this miserable fate for an excruciatingly long time.

The final part of verse 3 and verses 7, 9a–b, 9c draw four conclusions. The first is presented in verses 3f–6: a stillborn baby – which does not have to endure what the hypothetical person in Qoheleth's thought experiment has to go through – is better off. Qoheleth introduces his conclusion with the phrase *then I would say,* which marks what follows as a quasi-scientific deduction based on the evidence collected from his thought experiment. Although everything in Qoheleth's extended monologue is of course performed in spoken words, here the public orator Qoheleth marks his words as 'direct speech', for dramatic impact: *a stillborn baby is better off than him!* Most interpreters take Qoheleth literally (e.g. Longman 1998: 177; Bartholomew 2009: 318–319).

The idea that a stillborn baby (*nāpel*) is somehow better off than a living human being who has to endure relentless misery is a traditional biblical motif (Jer. 20:14–18; Job 3:1–26). Characters who compare a stillborn baby favourably with themselves are enduring extreme pain over a long time, and it is the *absence of pain* for stillborn children that makes their fate appear so attractive.

Psalm 58:8 [MT 58:9] makes a different point: 'Let them be . . . like a stillborn child that never sees the sun!' The reference to a stillborn child here serves several rhetorical purposes. It functions to emphasize the intensity of ill-will which the psalmist harbours for his enemies, it serves to insult those enemies and it functions to describe the severity of the punishment which the psalmist wishes upon them. We will come back to these observations shortly, when we will consider a possible double meaning attached to the term *stillborn baby*. Furthermore, and importantly, the fact that the psalmist mentions the circumstance that such a stillborn child has never seen the sun (*bal-ḥāzû šemeš*) is similar enough to Ecclesiastes 6:5a to warrant further exploration when we get to that verse below.

Qoheleth's language here is as exaggerated as the language of Jeremiah and Job. The comparison is not based on a psychological evaluation of the respective amounts of pain experienced by Job, Jeremiah and Qoheleth's test subject. Neither the stillborn child which never reached consciousness nor Qoheleth's fictional character ever experienced actual emotions. Qoheleth's point is a theoretical one, namely that *if* a person like the one he describes did exist, his fate would be one of relentless agony.

4. Qoheleth defends his first conclusion with six arguments. The first and second arguments come as a pair, as the stillborn baby's life cycle is described: *For in a mirage it comes, and into darkness it departs.* The poetically wistful metaphors highlight both the brevity and the illusory nature of the child that never came to be. The phrase evokes the heartache of those who lovingly yet vainly awaited its birth. Third, the child's anonymity is announced: *and in darkness its name is shrouded.* Why this apparently melancholy affirmation of the stillborn's social insignificance? Why the emphasis on the concealment of its identity? We will return to these questions shortly.

5. Fourth, we are informed, the miscarried child never had a visual or cognitive encounter with the sun: *also: the sun it has not seen or known.* We have reached Qoheleth's punchline. But what is so remarkable about it? If our interpretation of *sun* as a cypher for the occupying foreign power is correct, then Qoheleth here declares a stillborn child *happier* than the economically successful

Jewish collaborator who achieves all his material goals yet fails to enjoy them, because the stillborn child has never had to encounter the life-draining power of foreign rule.

The fifth reason for the stillborn's superiority is that it, rather than the collaborator, has *rest*, or perhaps better, 'peace of mind'. It may be that this statement has a particularly sharp edge because it would counter a possible argument by the collaborators, namely that their stance at least ensures *rest*, that is, absence of hostilities, for themselves and the Jewish community.

A review of these first five reasons reveals two strange circumstances. First, these statements are unsuited to a description of a stillborn child. Second, they are also mismatched as arguments in favour of a stillborn child's superior emotional state over against that of a living collaborator with conspicuous wealth, popularity, status, huge numbers of children and a supernaturally long life. This prompts us to consider the enigmatic statement regarding the stillborn child's concealed identity. Who, when compared with a collaborator, would be better off because his or her identity is kept secret? Surely not a miscarried child. Consequently, the term *stillborn baby* here is another cypher, a cryptograph for those who oppose foreign rule, ideologically, through passive resistance or as actual resistance activists.

The following is a rereading of the statements regarding the superiority of the emotional state of the *stillborn baby* – as a cypher for Jewish resistance fighters – over against that of the collaborator. Making a connection with the term 'stillborn child' in Psalm 58:8, where it was used pejoratively to imagine the deaths of the psalmist's enemies, representatives of the occupying forces and their Jewish supporters may have used the term as an insult. They may have used it with reference to the resistance fighters' subversive efforts, that they would never see the light of day, so to speak, and that their efforts would end with punishment by death. Perhaps they even referred to captured and killed partisans as 'miscarriages', trying to emphasize the futility of their efforts, the relative obscurity in which they may have died, and so on.

If this is so, then Qoheleth is countering this propaganda. He is suggesting that the stillborn child – read 'freedom fighter' – is better off than the collaborator. Freedom fighters come in disguise, hidden from sight (*in a mirage*, v. 4), and once their subversive task is complete they vanish under the cover of night (*into darkness*, v. 4). Their identity remains secret in order to avoid reprisals against their families (their name is shrouded in darkness, v. 4). They have not submitted to the coercion of the occupying powers (they have not seen or known the sun, v. 5a), and so they have a clear conscience and peace of mind, whether dead or alive (they have found rest, more than the collaborator, v. 5b).

6. The concluding sixth argument in support of Qoheleth's conclusion that a stillborn baby is somehow better off than the hypothetical person in Qoheleth's thought experiment also marks the conclusion of Qoheleth's quotation of himself introduced with *then I would say* back in verse 3. It reads like an interrupted afterthought: *and if there were a thousand years twice* [primary condition]*, but he cannot see goodness* [secondary condition] – . . . and here Qoheleth breaks off in the middle of the sentence.

After the protasis of this second conditional clause – which repeats in summary fashion some of the content of the first conditional clause in verse 3 – there should have been an apodosis. Why does Qoheleth break off mid-sentence? His oral mode of performance suggests that he expects his audience to complete the sentence for themselves, mentally filling the ellipsis with the nearest phrase that fits, such as *[then] a stillborn baby is better off than him* from verse 3.

It is almost certain that Qoheleth paused at this point in his spoken word delivery, in order to prompt his audience to finish the sentence for him. Dramatically, it is into the suspenseful gap created by the pause that he completes the final part of his self-quotation, in the form of a rhetorical question: *do they not all go to one place?* And again, the rhetorical question, which has its answer encoded through the way he designed it, prompts the audience to supply it for themselves: 'Yes, they do, and so do we!'

Qoheleth's persuasive strategy demands active participation from the audience. They cannot escape the conclusion to which Qoheleth has led them all along, namely that one day they too will die. The rhetorical effect is immense, for Qoheleth's audience is forced to conclude that they had better not follow the example of the rich but miserable collaborator, for who wants to be worse off than a stillborn child? The subversive potential of this rhetorical strategy is enormous: while those who actively resist the foreign powers may die before long, the alternative is a long life in misery. In this light, risking imminent death for the cause becomes an attractive alternative to collaboration.

7. Qoheleth seems to move on to a new topic, yet what follows is still somehow connected: it is the second conclusion from the hypothetical scenario described back in verse 3. This technique is a mainstay of modern stand-up comedians, in which the audience is left wondering whether or not the performer has really moved on, or whether he or she is still talking about the same subject but approaching it from a new angle. The latter is the case here.

Abruptly, or so it seems, Qoheleth makes another startling claim: *All the hard work of the man is for his mouth, and yet the throat is never filled.* The thought is not directly connected to what has gone just before, but three reasons suggest a connection nonetheless. First, its content is reminiscent of verse 3d: *but his throat is not filled from this good.* Second, four of the seven appearances of the noun *nepeš, throat,* in the book of Ecclesiastes occur right here (6:2, 3, 7, 9). It is a catchword, another classic tool of stand-up comedians. Third, the definite article in *hā'ādām, the man,* suggests that the person being talked about here has already been mentioned. Consequently, it must be the *'îš, man,* of verses 2 and 3 whose *throat* has not been filled, just like the *throat* of the man here. Thus Qoheleth turns the apparently universal claim of verse 7 into a sarcastic verdict on the greedy collaborator of verses 1–6, exposing all in one sweep both the self-centred motivation for his keen effort to get ahead in life and the irony of it, making the man look foolish and his efforts tragically misguided, futile and ridiculous.

8. The causal particle *For* signals that the following two rhetorical questions and their implied answers support the argument of the preceding material, all the way from verse 1 to verse 7. The first question reads: *what advantage to the wise man over the fool?* and implies a negative reply. Scholars frequently draw attention to Proverbs 16:26 in order to provide a framework for its interpretation: 'A labourer's throat toils for him, for his mouth urges him.' The comparison of the wise with the fool may reflect an internal Jewish debate over the intellectual superiority of those who accommodated themselves to the foreign overlords. In this line of thinking, only fools would fail to take advantage, they might claim. They might even have a slogan to promote their values, such as 'Profit for the wise over the fool, profit for the wise over the fool, profit for the wise over the fool!'

There are other proverbs, however, which are equally relevant. Among these are several so-called 'better' proverbs, similar in form to the phrase here, where less income in favour of intellectual, religious or ethical virtues is celebrated: 'Better a little with fear of the Lord than great wealth and terror with it' (Prov. 15:16); or 'Better a little in righteousness than great gain without justice' (Prov. 16:8). Consequently, Qoheleth is not opposed to intellectual virtues as such, but he is attacking a new form of foreign wisdom devoid of the traditional Jewish values of fear of the Lord and social justice. In line with verse 7, then, Qoheleth here addresses the lack of satisfaction *in spite of material affluence* because the absence of traditional Jewish virtues (fear of the Lord, justice) annuls the satisfaction one might otherwise have experienced. It is as if he provocatively quotes the would-be collaborators' own slogan back at them: *What* 'profit for the wise over the fool'?

This line of thought continues with the second question: *what [. . .] for the poor who know how to advance in life/against the living?* Three aspects of the phrase complicate matters. (1) The word *yôter* from the first part of the verse is implied through ellipsis. (2) The final word *haḥayyim* is ambiguous, for it can mean 'life' or 'the living'. In view of the article, the latter meaning is more likely, but the ambiguity is almost certainly intentional. (3) The combination of the verb *hlk* followed by the unusual preposition *neged* + *haḥayyim* as indirect object needs interpretation. It has two meanings, depending on whether one takes *haḥayyim* to refer to 'life' or to 'the living'. With the former meaning, the phrase means 'how to get on in life', 'how to cope with life', that is, how to be successful in overcoming life's challenges. With the latter meaning, the phrase means 'how to advance against the living', in the sense of how to be more successful than others with whom one competes. The word *'āni, poor,* and the phrase *who know how to advance in life/against the living* are expressions that belong to the world of competitive commerce. This articulates the idea, surely tempting for many of Qoheleth's contemporaries, that the new climate under foreign rule provided new opportunities for everybody, including the poor. If they were smart enough (*ḥākām*) to take advantage (*yôter*) of the new elite's need for collusion from the indigenous population, then the poor, too, could make it rich. Perhaps people were even citing their poverty as justification for their willingness to collaborate. This, too, may have been a popular slogan: 'For the poor who know how to get on in life!'

Against the preceding case studies, however, Qoheleth reaffirms that even the poor who have the skill to take advantage of the situation will end up rich and disappointed (6:1–7), and so their apparent advance brings them no real success at all. This question, too, then, takes on the tinge of a tease, turning the would-be collaborators' slogan against them: *What* 'for the poor who know how to get on in life'?

9. Against their slogans, however, Qoheleth proposes one of his own: *Better the seeing of the eyes than the wandering of the throat!* This counter-slogan challenges the earlier ones and returns to the promotion of moderation in 5:8–12 and of economic self-restraint in 5:18–20. Longman's take on the verse, '[t]he general idea of the proverb is that what is present in hand is much better than what one only desires but does not have' (Longman 1998: 175), gets to the heart of the matter. It applies to Qoheleth's overall strategy to promote modesty over unrealistic ambition all the way from 5:8 to 6:9, and it provides the third conclusion from the hypothetical scenario described back in verse 3.

The evaluative refrain *This, too, is a mirage and a chasing after wind!* offers the fourth conclusion from the hypothetical scenario described back in verse 3 and brings the entire discourse of 5:8 – 6:9 to a close. The entity under evaluation is uncertain because here, too, the referent of the demonstrative pronoun is unclear. It could refer to the second part of the proverb in verse 9a (*the wandering of the throat*), it could refer to the 'better' proverb in verse 9a as a whole (*Better the seeing of the eyes than the wandering of the throat!*) or it could refer to the desire of wealth as such (so Longman).

Meaning
The last appearance of the evaluative refrain occurred in 4:16, and the pursuit of happiness through material affluence is the central

theme in the larger segment of Qoheleth's spoken word performance from 5:1 to 6:6. Consequently, this theme, covered across the material, is the referent of the demonstrative pronoun. Qoheleth has debunked the idea that success or happiness (= *yitrôn*) can be gained through material affluence, exposing it as a mirage and a chasing after wind.

Since the next verses (6:10–12) form a programmatic reflection drawing conclusions from the four case studies that precede it and introducing the following material on practical wisdom, we will explore the *Meaning* of Case Studies 8 and 9 in more detail at the end of those verses.

16. A REFLECTION ON THE HUMAN CONDITION IN THE LIGHT OF CASE STUDIES 6–9 (6:10–12)

Context

Qoheleth's second interlude (cf. the first, in 5:18–20) presents a reflection on the human condition in the light of Case Studies 6–9 in 5:13 – 6:9, which have sought to demonstrate that the pursuit of happiness through material affluence is a mirage.

Comment

10. The reflection opens with what sounds like a programmatic statement. The phrase *Whatever has occurred* refers to events that have recently taken place, atrocities that have been committed in Judea by the occupying forces, acts of suppression and exploitation. The allusion is so faint that it would have been easy to miss. Just in case, therefore, Qoheleth drops a hint: *its name has already been called.* The phrase is usually taken to refer to God's creative acts in Genesis 1. This is intentional, for Qoheleth does not want to be too obvious. What he is *really* talking about, however, are conditions *under the sun*, the foreign exploitation tactics (4:1) and atrocities (4:3). And the name he has given to these occurrences is his cypher for the occupying power, the cryptogram *under the sun*. This is confirmed by the next phrase, which reinforces the point: *and it is known what that is*. He is, of course, referring to his cypher for the foreign rule.

The phrase can be and has been taken differently, for the next word, *'ādām* (*man*), can either be read as the last word of that phrase ('and it is known what human beings are'; so most commentators), or it can be read as the first word of the following phrase. The hinge function of the word creates deliberate ambiguity to dodge accusations of sedition. And this next phrase, with or without *'ādām* at its head, continues the rhetorical ducking and diving. It can also be read in two ways. It states that someone *cannot win a case against one who is stronger than him*, and the stronger one either can be God (so a broad consensus), or it can refer to the occupying foreign regime. The phrase is hyper-ambiguous, as usual. Qoheleth appears to claim that nobody can change divinely ordained realities. In reality, he alludes to the repressive policies under foreign rule.

11. The phrase *ki yēš* asserts the existence or truthfulness of the statement it introduces. *For it is true: 'the more words, the more elaborate the mirage.'* Whose words? The underdetermined expression with its striking alliteration signals a proverb. This means that it is a free-floating rhetorical tool that can be used to critique whatever 'words' the proverb is used to evaluate. Since Qoheleth uses the proverb to comment on the preceding verse, the *děbārim harbēh* most naturally refers to the words used to *win a case against* superior powers. Qoheleth uses the proverb to bolster the veracity of his claim in verse 10, namely that neither he nor his audience have the power to change political realities. Again, Qoheleth uses ambiguity to veil his subversive talk. The attempt to challenge the status quo is futile, no matter how hard one tries. And this is expressed in the rhetorical question that brings verse 11 to a close: *What advantage for the man?*

12. The next part of the defence consists of two rhetorical questions. The first reads *who knows what is good for the man . . . ?* It is a two-in-one question. The base-level question is 'What is *good* for the man?' The top-level question is 'Who knows?' It is worth pausing to remember that the implied answer does not deny that there may be something good for the man. What is denied is that anyone knows what that good is.

Here is the description of the sphere of life in which something good is sought: *the number of the days of the life of his mirage, which he has made like the shadow.* Qoheleth talks about the prevailing conditions under foreign occupation. The elaborate construct chain *the number of the days of the life of his mirage* emphasizes that every day of the man's life is an enactment of the mirage that he has constructed for the prevailing conditions. The final phrase, *which he has made like the shadow*, goes even further and refines the idea of the man's life being a mirage with the related image of each of his days being *like the shadow*, a graphic addition to the visual metaphors *mirage* and *under the sun*.

Returning now to the rhetorical question *who knows what is good . . . under the sun?*, it is clear that the negative answer – implied through its rhetorical formulation – suggests that nobody, not even the man himself, knows the correct response to the question that is on everybody's mind: what is the right thing to do in response to foreign occupation and exploitation?

The strangely placed relative pronoun *which* that links this question with the next befuddles modern interpreters so much that they act as if it was simply not there. The random placement of the relative pronoun can be explained as a feature of Qoheleth's spoken word performance. Perhaps he left a pregnant pause after the end of the first rhetorical question, giving his audience a chance to supply the implied answer: 'Nobody.' And into the silence he dropped his isolated *which*, thus raising the expectation that what follows is intimately linked.

The phrase *who will tell the man what will be after him under the sun?* then poses the second rhetorical question. Again, the implied answer is, 'Nobody.' The claim that no-one can know the future is neither controversial nor remarkable. Even though the ancient world knew of ways to divine the future (through hepatoscopy, astrology, and consultation of oracles or the dead), knowing the future was universally considered something that was beyond the grasp of normal human beings without special training or access to the divine. This insight was not unique and original to Qoheleth. It is a banality, something that everybody already agreed with. Qoheleth here, too, is making a polemical and political rather than a philosophical point. The rhetorical question implies that nobody is able to tell anyone in the Jewish community how things will turn out with the occupying powers. The section is framed by similar phrases at the beginning and end which refer to the past (*whatever has occurred*) and the future (*what will be*) under foreign rule (see Krüger 2004: 132). Qoheleth and his community are uncertain about how best to respond to atrocities that have occurred in the recent past, and they lack certainty over how to plan their response in view of the occupying power's unpredictability.

Meaning
Case Studies 6–9 and the programmatic reflection which follows them do relate to the divine ordering of the world, but only superficially. The world in which Qoheleth and his Jewish compatriots live is in dire straits, and it is God who enforces the status quo. The responsibility for the prevailing circumstances, however, lies elsewhere: it lies on the shoulders of the Jewish population. God has allowed the exile and a series of subsequent occupations by foreign powers in response to Judea's sins. It also lies on the shoulders of the foreign occupiers, who continue to enforce their supremacy violently, if necessary.

From now on, Qoheleth's speech sequence relates ever more directly to the political situation under foreign rule.

17. FOURTH PRACTICAL INTERLUDE: INSTRUCTION ON COPING WITH BEREAVEMENT (7:1–14)

Context

In his fourth practical interlude, Qoheleth addresses his community as they are gathered for the funeral of someone who may have been killed by the foreign regime. In the emotionally charged atmosphere, he addresses three main issues: (1) the discouragement and pain of the bereaved family and wider community; (2) the seething resentment and anger of those present; (3) the disillusionment and resigned fatalism of others. He begins with advice in the form of six maxims (vv. 1, 2, 3, 5, 8a, 8b), followed by five instructions (vv. 9–14).

There is little connection to earlier parts of Qoheleth's speech, because with chapter 7, Qoheleth's discourse changes substantially from a sequence of case studies on general issues to case studies and practical advice on specific issues. It is for this reason that only three of the ten occurrences of the word *yitrôn* (7:12; 10:10–11) appear in the second half of the speech (chs. 7–12). The structure and literary form of this part of Qoheleth's speech is loose, but the occasion of a bereavement visit or funeral would have bound the sequence into a coherent spoken reflection, with the audience supplying the contextual links from one pronouncement to the next.

Comment

1. What follows are six maxims on coping with bereavement. The first maxim consists of two complementary 'better' sayings which categorically declare a person's good reputation (*Better a name*) to be more important than wealth, luxury and pleasure (*than good oil*). In the Hebrew, the word *ṭôb* ('good, better') is omitted but implied twice in this one verse. First, it is implied in the collocation 'good name', but it is not repeated because it already appears as the comparative. Second, it is implied as the comparative at the beginning of the second 'better' saying. The similarity with Proverbs 22:1 ('A good name is more choice than great wealth, being valued [is better] than silver and gold') is striking, but Qoheleth's version has much more punch, and the context points to the explosive sociopolitical situation under foreign rule.

The sequence is more than an abstract, melancholic meditation on life's end; it speaks into the concrete situation of a recent bereavement. The loss of life may have resulted from an explosive incident, perhaps in the form of retaliation against political unrest. The deceased may have been one of those freedom fighters cryptically called a *stillborn baby* in 6:3.

Into such a context of grief and public mourning, and of raw emotions, the words *Better a name than good oil* (note the soothing sequence of similar sounds in Hebrew) remind the mourning community that the deceased has not died in vain. In contrast with a detested collaborator, who may have gained *good oil* (a metaphor for wealth and luxury, what Qoheleth consistently calls *a mirage*), the deceased had gained more: *a name* – that is, a good name, honoured by the community.

For someone who gave his life for the welfare of the community, the *day of death* is indeed better *than the day of his birth* (the personal pronoun refers to the actual person being mourned by the community).

2. Qoheleth offers a second maxim, also in the form of a 'better' saying: *Better to go to a house of mourning than to go to a house of feasting.* The occasion is the funeral of someone who has been killed because of his resistance to the foreign regime. The comparison is between the funeral of a hero and the feasting of collaborators with the foreign overlords. Against this background, the two-pronged defence of Qoheleth's startling claim takes on a new meaning. First, the supporting argument *for that is the end of every human being* takes on a comforting quality. If death does indeed ultimately come to all human beings, then the tragic end of the life celebrated here is a little easier to bear, and for this reason Qoheleth urges his audience to apply that knowledge to their situation: *and the living should take it to heart.*

3. Murphy opens his comment on this verse laconically: 'An obscure verse in itself and in context' (Murphy 1992: 64). Other scholars are equally puzzled (Longman 1998: 183; Krüger 2004: 136). The general bewilderment may be resolved through its inter-pretation against the explosive situation under foreign rule. The term *ka'as* ('grief, resentment') fits well into a context where Qoheleth's bereaved community mourn the death of one of their own at the hands of foreigners and collaborators. No wonder their anguished sorrow turns to bitter resentment against those whom they hold responsible for their loss. Qoheleth in fact stokes the fire in this third maxim: *Better resentment than laughter,* he counsels, *for through badness of face the heart becomes good.* Embracing one's anger in the face of bloody injustice is preferable to suppressing it. This contextual interpretation, therefore, does not clash with other statements about *ka'as* ('grief, resentment') elsewhere in Qoheleth's discourse (e.g. 5:17). The justification for this inflammatory claim suggests that the public expression of anger (*through badness of face*) has a cathartic and healing effect on the emotions (*the heart becomes good*). The wordplay on something 'good' emerging from something 'bad' gives the verse a counter-intuitive, paradoxical and thus thought-provoking quality that accurately reflects the bewilderment that invariably accompanies the violent death of a loved one. Is Qoheleth inciting violence? More likely, his advice aims to provide a 'pressure valve' to relieve the seething resentment among the funeral party (cf. v. 9).

4. Presented in the form of a traditional proverb, two complementary statements may serve several purposes at once: *The heart of the wise is in the house of mourning, but the heart of fools is in the house of joy.* This can be taken in isolation from the actual event of a burial (Longman 1998: 184). However, the repetition of the catchword *heart* from verse 3 indicates a direct connection with the preceding statement, and thus connects the proverb to an actual funeral. Qoheleth encourages his audience to adopt the actions of the types of persons who have wise hearts and who may, for example, help the funeral guests to refrain from retaliation. Additionally, the proverb may reassure the community that their choice to be present at the funeral signals their wisdom, and conversely may condemn as fools those who have chosen to be elsewhere, perhaps at a party with the occupying forces.

5. The series of maxims reaches an initial climax, for Qoheleth supports his fourth maxim with no fewer than three justifications, all in striking language. In another 'better' saying, the less attractive form of communication comes from an attractive source – it is *the rebuke of a wise person* – while the more attractive form of communication comes from an unattractive source – *a song of fools*. The saying's emphasis lies on discouraging people from following the attractive songs of fools at the expense of the improvement available through the correction offered by a wise counsellor. The saying's contextual function in Qoheleth's oratory is crucial. This is a carefully crafted routine, not an impromptu talk, despite its occasional character. The focus in verses 5–7 is practical: Qoheleth urges the members of a funeral party to heed his own wise counsel as recorded in the following verses. The next two verses present three arguments in favour of the evaluation, which in effect is an indirect directive.

6. The first argument is introduced with the causal particle *For*. Qoheleth then compares *the laughter of the fool* to *the sound of thorns under the pot* (*kĕqôl hassirim tahat hassir*). The phrase has two ingenious wordplays: (1) The word *šîr*, *song*, from verse 5 is matched with the final word *hassîr*, *the pot*, here. The two words are near-homophones. (2) Within verse 6, there are two words that look alike in the Hebrew, although they have different meanings. The words are homographs, words that are spelled the same (*hassîr* = 'the pot'; *hassîrîm* = 'the thorns') and in Qoheleth's performance sound the same. The effect is impressive and entertaining. The sound of the crackling thorns under a pot is attractive, similar to human laughter. But the burning thorns would be useless for heating the food in the pot. And what is more, explosively burning thorns would create a fire hazard (in the case of indoor cooking). Thus the following aspects are prominent in the comparison: (1) its entertaining nature; (2) its ineffectiveness in providing what it should (heat in the case of thorns, happiness in the case of laughter); (3) its combustible nature (to cause fire in the case of thorns, to cause strife or worse in the case of the laughter of the fool). The phrase *And this also is a mirage* provides the second justification and refers to the negative statements in verses 4b, 5b and 6b: to foolish joy, foolish song and foolish laughter.

7. The word *For* signals a third justification for the statement in verse 5. A striking admission, *the oppression can fool a wise man*, is complemented with the statement *and a gift can destroy a heart*. A contextual interpretation integrates the verse with the preceding maxims. The definite article in *the oppression* indicates that Qoheleth is addressing the sociopolitical situation at hand – oppression at the hands of the foreign overlords (cf. 5:8). His words come as a timely warning that those who deem themselves *wise* as they partake of the *good oil* (v. 1), visit *a house of feasting* (v. 2), laugh off the grief of their community in the *house of joy* (vv. 3a, 4b) and seek distraction from present realities through entertainment, the *song* of verse 5b, are fooling themselves. Qoheleth challenges what they consider to be *wise*, namely their attempt to make the best of the opportunities offered through the foreign overlords. Their scheme to get the best of both worlds will turn them into fools: *the oppression can fool a wise man*. The 'present' with which the new regime lures them will cost them their integrity and their happiness: *and a gift can destroy a heart*.

8. Two complementary 'better' sayings, Qoheleth's fifth and sixth maxims, transition Qoheleth's talk to a new focus, similar to the transitions from one topic to another in the routines of modern stand-up comedians. The previous sequence had challenged those who were prone to assimilation with the new regime. This new sequence, which runs until verse 14, aims to calm the hotheads.

The first saying concerns the advantage of hindsight: *Better is the end of a word/matter than its beginning.* The saying carries several meanings, designed to entertain and instruct all at once, due to the multivalence of the word *dābār*, which can mean 'word' or 'matter', and because it lacks an obvious referent. (1) It may refer to the opening of Qoheleth's talk, to verse 1b. Then it would mean something like 'The end of human life is better than its beginning' – especially the life of a martyr. (2) It may be a comment on the progression of Qoheleth's own monologue, something like 'The coming part of my talk is even more important than its beginning'. (3) The word *dābār* may refer to the sociopolitical situation as a whole, the oppression under which Qoheleth and his community live. Then it would mean something like 'The end of this period of oppression will be better than its beginning'. (4) It may refer to the specific situation at hand, namely the events leading up to the funeral and its consequences for the community. Then it would mean something like 'The final outcome of this terrible tragedy will be better than its beginning'.

The ambiguity is deliberate and effective, as the diverse interpretations which the phrase has received over time demonstrate (see the brief review in Longman 1998: 187). It contributes to Qoheleth's persuasive strategy and creates plausible deniability.

The sixth maxim offers another example of Qoheleth's clever wordplays, aimed to poke fun at the targets of his jibes. The Hebrew *ṭôb 'erek-rûaḥ miggĕbah-rûaḥ* is another example of an entire phrase with several meanings, a caustically funny proverb which was almost certainly coined for the occasion by Qoheleth himself. Literally it says, *better a long wind [rûaḥ] than a high wind [rûaḥ]*. The Bible versions and subsequent interpreters take *rûaḥ* here as referring to a person's disposition, and use paraphrases like 'spirit' to indicate this. Consequently, the usual interpretation given to the proverb is 'patience over pride' (e.g. Murphy 1992: 65). They miss that Qoheleth, not for the first time, is having fun with the other meaning of *rûaḥ* as *wind* (cf. 5:16, where *rûaḥ* alluded to flatulence).

Four interpretive constellations emerge: (1) 'better a long wind than a high wind', a literal translation that showcases the proverb's ambiguity, leaving open what *wind* means in each instance; (2) 'better a long wind than an arrogant spirit', a semi-traditional interpretation that emphasizes the ambiguous nature of *'erek-rûaḥ*; (3) 'better a patient spirit than an arrogant spirit', the traditional interpretation; (4) 'better a patient spirit than a high wind', the primary meaning-constellation that Qoheleth wants his audience to discover. In this understanding, the idea of a 'high wind' does not denote arrogance or pride, but a storm, as in the English idiom 'high wind and weather', with the storm operating as an emblem for political trouble. The four meaning-constellations emerge all at once, and this is how Qoheleth wants it. The complex play on words mimics the complexity of the situation that Qoheleth's community faces, and it does so in an entertaining way, challenging and encouraging his audience to think carefully about the best course of action under the circumstances. This is confirmed by the following verses, where Qoheleth warns against vexation and political confrontation.

9. Verse 9 constitutes the first of five instructions in verses 9–14, all intended to help the funeral guests control their anger and avoid violent clashes with the foreigners.

Most interpreters see a direct clash between verse 9 and verse 3 (Krüger 2004: 137). Yet the tension between the statements in verses 1–7 and those in verses 8–14 arises from the actual context, the funeral gathering at which Qoheleth addresses two complementary concerns related to his community's welfare. In verses 1–7 he is challenging those tempted to assimilate with the new regime, whereas in verses 8–14 he is cautioning those ready to rise up. The phrase *Do not hurry in your spirit to become vexed* picks up the mention of *'erek-rûah* in verse 8 and counsels the gathering to resist the emotional impulse generated by the occasion. Qoheleth then defends his instruction by drawing attention to the folly of unrestrained anger: *for vexation lodges in the lap of fools.* Anger tends to cloud clear thinking, leading to foolish rebellion against more powerful opponents.

10. A second instruction, in the form of the prohibition *Do not say . . . !*, introduces what he knows they are thinking already: *How is it that the former days were better than these?* This is a question born out of wistful nostalgia that romanticizes a distant past free from foreign rule and resentfully blows the negative aspects of the present situation out of all proportion. The direct quotation verbalizes what many are thinking and dramatizes the intensity of their resentment. The following material presents two sophisticated arguments in support of Qoheleth's prohibition. The first argument is a provocative claim: *for it is not out of wisdom that you enquire about this!*

11. This argument is, of course, no more than an assertion, so Qoheleth now explains why it is so: *A good thing is wisdom with an inheritance, and an advantage for those who continue to see the sun.* Confusion has arisen over the connection between *wisdom* and *naḥălâ* ('inheritance', 'property'). The preposition *'im* which connects them can mean 'with', 'as good as', 'in comparison with'. The most common translation is 'wisdom is good with property' (Longman 1998: 189–190). My interpretation departs from traditional attempts. Qoheleth's explanation makes more sense if all of it is heard at once, if it is understood against its sociopolitical background under foreign rule and if *naḥălâ* is understood as *inheritance* in the sense of what a deceased person leaves behind for his family (cf. Ruth 4:5, 10). A wisdom that refuses to indulge in nostalgia (v. 10) that leads to either despair or insurgence will help people keep their property to pass on to their posterity, and this is *an advantage* (*yōter*, same Hebrew root as *yitrôn*) for those who have to continue to subsist under foreign rule (*and an advantage for those who continue to see the sun*).

12. The second argument opens with another enigmatic assertion: *For in the shadow of wisdom, in the shadow of silver.* Qoheleth may be using a proverb to suggest, in the first part of the argument, that wise restraint (cf. vv. 8–11) provides a shelter from the harmful rays of *the sun*, that is, foreign coercion. The second part suggests that *silver* (= money) also has the capacity to provide shelter from *the sun*, but then continues this thought in the remainder of the verse: *but the success of knowing this wisdom is this: it keeps its owners alive.* In other words, if Qoheleth's audience heed his advice, their wisdom will keep them alive because they will avoid violent confrontation with the foreign regime.

13. Qoheleth presents and defends his third instruction: *See the work of God.* The instruction links back to 1:15 and anticipates 7:29. It urges Qoheleth's audience to step back from the immediate situation and reflect on the theological origin of their predicament. It provides a theological justification for his community's affliction under foreign rule. He implies that it has been brought about by God. And so, if the present situation is indeed a consequence of continuing divine judgment, there is nothing that the community can do about it, as the answer implied in the rhetorical question suggests: *for who can straighten what he has made crooked?* Nobody can, not even through violence.

14. Qoheleth presents his fourth instruction, to enjoy the good times as and when they occur: *On a good day, enjoy the good.* This is not just about making do with whatever comes, but is an encouragement to make the best of every opportunity to find happiness. Qoheleth's fifth instruction does not urge 'making the best of a bad day' (Longman 1998: 192). Rather, the phrase *on a bad day* introduces the circumstances under which Qoheleth advises his audience to consider that God has made not only the good day, but also the bad day: *God made that day also, just as he made the other* (cf. Job 1:21).

The prepositional phrase *'al-dibrat še-* is rare and enigmatic. Three interpretations have been proposed: (1) It may mean 'so that' and thus introduce the intention behind God's work, namely to ensure that *the man cannot find anything that will come after him.* But the statement seems to have little sense. (2) The expression may employ an idiom known in Syriac, where 'to find something after' means 'to find fault with', a meaning that appears to be reflected in Symmachus ('that man may not find complaint against him'; Murphy 1992: 61, 66; Whitley 1979: 66). The usage here in Ecclesiastes would be a so-called 'calque', a loan translation from Syriac with the meaning 'so that man may not find any fault with him [= God]'. (3) The phrase may have causal force, with the meaning 'for', 'because' (Krüger 2004: 134–135). This proposal may prompt the objection that Qoheleth could simply have used the normal particle *kî* if he wanted to express causality. In response, it seems likely that he chose the longer phrase for emphasis. Consequently, the phrase should be translated: *on account of the fact that the man cannot find out anything about the future.* The circumstance that the man cannot know the future justifies Qoheleth's giving of the preceding two instructions. He urges his audience to accept the alternation of good and bad times in life as a divinely ordered reality to motivate them to enjoy the good times in life on the one hand, while accepting without bitterness the inevitable difficult periods in life on the other. This was especially important while Judea continued to suffer foreign interference, even after the Babylonian

exile. Qoheleth implies that the continuing quasi-exilic circumstances were imposed by God, that the future is uncertain, and that
his community should neither allow themselves to slide into
fatalistic resignation nor let themselves be goaded into violent
resistance.

Meaning
These verses plausibly fit into the ˙situation of a community
occupied by a foreign power, with the particular occasion being a
memorial celebration for someone who had recently been killed by
the foreigners.

Oppressive circumstances like these tend to prompt three kinds
of responses: (1) collaboration with the occupying forces, addressed
in verses 1–8; (2) fatalistic resignation and cultural as well as
religious assimilation, addressed in the entire sequence; (3) violent
retaliation, addressed in verses 9–14. Qoheleth's advice has the capacity to inform the response of entire communities in complex and
explosive political circumstances today.

18. FIFTH PRACTICAL INTERLUDE: INSTRUCTION ON COPING WITH THE LACK OF A DIRECT CORRELATION BETWEEN ACTS AND THEIR CONSEQUENCES (7:15–22)

Context

This practical interlude concerns human failure to control life's circumstances despite wisdom and righteousness. The reference to ten rulers in the city links the reflection to the sociopolitical circumstances under foreign rule. As a direct consequence of foreign interference in the community's internal affairs, life had become unpredictable. Qoheleth's community had lost control over their own affairs, irrespective of their members' wisdom and righteousness. Qoheleth urges his audience to re-evaluate ancient Jewish wisdom perspectives, according to which wisdom and righteousness lead to a long, healthy and happy life, in the light of the fact that arbitrary acts by members of the occupying regime with their foreign legal norms may randomly interrupt and thwart traditional expectations.

This part of the speech sequence is only loosely connected with what precedes and what follows. It is an independent reflection whose connection with its literary environment lies in the adverse sociopolitical circumstances of Jewish life under foreign occupation, which dominate all of the material.

Comment

15. Qoheleth abruptly changes the topic, introducing it with a summary statement on past experience. The phrase *I have seen it all* (*'et-hakkōl rā'iti*) sounds as disheartened in Hebrew as it does in English translation. The next phrase – *in the days of my mirage* – refers to a time when he himself had bought into a mirage from whose influence he now wants to deliver his audience. This is what he had seen: *the case of a righteous man who perished in his righteousness, and the case of a wicked man who prolonged [his life] in his wickedness.* The introduction suggests that what he observed was incongruous with the illusory worldview under whose influence he was then living.

Possibly this illusory (*hebel*) worldview was the assumption that good people will always experience good things (the righteous live long and happy lives), while bad things happen only to bad people (the wicked will live short and miserable lives) (cf. Kushner 1981). However, the inseparable preposition *bĕ-* can mean 'in spite of' or 'because of' (Krüger 2004: 140; Waltke and O'Connor 1990: §12.2.5d–e): some people may have died prematurely *because* of their righteousness (or wisdom), and some people may have prolonged their lives *because* of their wickedness (or folly). The ambiguity is almost certainly intentional, and so the traditional interpretation – that Qoheleth is describing his disillusionment with the belief in a direct connection between deeds and their consequences – cannot be sustained. In the context of Qoheleth's regime-critical monologue, this is not only an abstract observation on the moral fabric of human existence, but also a comment on the legal realities of the day, when normal rules no longer apply.

16. In verses 16–22 Qoheleth explores four possible responses to the lack of direct correlation between acts and their consequences. The first two of these verses (vv. 16–17) are expressed in similar fashion, which indicates that the two instructions are related in meaning, complementing each other. Together, they aim to discourage two extreme sets of responses to legal uncertainty.

In verse 16 Qoheleth offers and defends the first of his four instructions on how to respond to the circumstance that sometimes bad things happen to good people and good things happen to bad people: *Do not be overly righteous and do not pretend to be excessively wise!* The occurrence of exceptions to the rule does not mean that there is no rule at all. Qoheleth's advice aims at genuinely righteous and wise behaviour enriched with the important insight that exceptions to the rule do happen (Krüger 2004: 140). He wants to discourage extreme responses like legal and intellectual perfectionism, as if super-righteousness or supreme wisdom were able to restore the rule's universal validity. Verse 19 with its pointed – perhaps even defiant – preference for wisdom over *ten rulers* suggests the possibility that Qoheleth is also talking about the different legal standards held by foreign officials, including their potentially inconsistent, random and arbitrary application in matters relating to legal concerns of the local population. Qoheleth is urging his fellow citizens to adopt a stance in legal matters that takes account of these circumstances. On the one hand, they are not to take the legal standards imposed by foreign rule too literally (*Do not be overly righteous*). On the other hand, he encourages them not to try to outsmart the foreign legal system (*and do not pretend to be excessively wise*). Neither of these coping strategies is capable of restoring the rule's universal validity.

Qoheleth uses a pointedly crisp rhetorical question – *Why harm yourself?* – to support his instruction. Its implied answer – that there is no good reason whatsoever why one would want to put oneself into such a position – supports all of the above interpretations. Nonetheless, the regime-critical interpretation is boosted considerably through the ambivalence of the verb *šmm*. A prominent facet of the verb's meaning concerns social isolation, the sense of being physically and emotionally removed or isolated from contact with other people due to adverse circumstances (see esp. 2 Sam. 13:20; Isa. 54:1; Lam. 3:11). In the passive-reflexive *hitpolel* form in Ecclesiastes 7:16, then, it may refer to social self-isolation. What Qoheleth is really asking is: 'Why would you want to exclude yourself from the community through such behaviour?'

17. Qoheleth offers and defends the second of his four instructions on how to respond to legal uncertainty: *Do not be overly wicked, and don't be a dupe!* This second instruction complements the first by discouraging a response among his audience that swings to the other extreme, from super-compliance to rebellion, whether against social, ethical and legal norms in general or the compromised legal system imposed by the foreign regime in particular.

The last of these four prohibitions uses an unusual term for 'fool', the rare noun *sākāl* (only here and in 2:19; 10:3, 14). It also is unqualified. Interpreters regularly draw attention to this fact. Longman is representative in drawing two conclusions: first, Qoheleth appears to suggest that folly should be avoided completely, as opposed to righteousness, wisdom and wickedness, which apparently are commended or at least permitted in moderation. Second, the qualified prohibition of wickedness 'leaves open the possibility of a "reasonable" level of wickedness' (Longman 1998: 196).

An alternative explanation makes better sense of the two unusual features of the last prohibition: it is not an independent prohibition of folly, but it explains and focuses the previous prohibition to refrain from excessive wickedness. To paraphrase its pragmatic-rhetorical impact, Qoheleth is saying: 'Do not be overly wicked and thereby fool yourself!' Even in the current situation where the legal system is flawed, Qoheleth is suggesting, an openly rebellious reaction would be self-destructively foolish. With the general population, such a rebel against moral norms will isolate him- or herself from the community. This person will suffer a social death, so to speak. With the occupying forces, however, the consequences are likely to be more severe. It may cost the person his or her life, as suggested in the rhetorical question *Why die when it is not your time?* with which Qoheleth supports his instruction.

18. Qoheleth presents his third instruction, which he then defends with two arguments. *It is good for you to hold fast to this and also not to let your hand go from that.* Although articulated in the form of an evaluative statement, it amounts to an instruction which reinforces the previous two by stressing that Qoheleth's audience should strike a balance between the first two instructions and follow both. Qoheleth's advice aims at genuinely righteous and wise behaviour enriched with the important insight that wisdom and righteousness do not guarantee success. Qoheleth promotes a mature kind of wisdom which leads to genuine righteousness, avoids ethical perfectionism and fosters realistic expectations.

The remainder of the verse presents Qoheleth's first argument in its favour: *For the one who fears God will come out of all these.* Fear of God in the Old Testament refers to reverent obedience to God.

The phrase promises that the God-fearer will escape all of the negative circumstances mentioned in verses 15–17: perishing in one's righteousness (v. 15), harming oneself (v. 16) and dying when it is not one's time (v. 17). The God-fearer who follows Qoheleth's advice will succeed, despite the legal uncertainties described in verse 15.

19. Qoheleth's second argument to support his instruction to act with genuine wisdom and righteousness drives home the point: *This wisdom is stronger for the wise man than ten rulers who are in the city.* The direct article at the beginning with the word *wisdom* functions as a demonstrative pronoun: *this* wisdom – that is, the wisdom commended by Qoheleth in the previous verses – makes a wise person stronger *than ten rulers who are in the city.* This unusually long and cumbersome description signals that Qoheleth is subversively referring to the foreign authorities in Jerusalem by means of a veiled allusion that allows him to deny wrongdoing. Qoheleth's wisdom enables God-fearers to overcome whatever challenges the legal system imposed by the foreign regime throws at them.

20. Qoheleth's justification for this bold claim, *for there is no man on earth so righteous that he [only] does good and never sins,* is not a universal assertion (but cf. Rom. 7:20). In the traditional interpretation, the particle *kî,* which usually has causal force, does not fit with the context. A contextual interpretation against the background of an oppressive legal system imposed by the foreign authorities, however, integrates it with the rest of Qoheleth's routine. He reassures his audience that the kinds of moral compromises which his advice necessitates are justifiable on the grounds that moral perfection is unobtainable at any rate, and so the legal ducking and diving which he commends under the circumstances can be defended on theological grounds.

21–22. Verses 21–22 offer and defend the fourth and final instruction in the series. However, while the first three of these were prompted by the circumstances described in verse 15, these two verses combine to form an afterthought on the theological comment about human beings in the preceding verse alone. Qoheleth gives what appears to be a rather puzzling instruction: *Also, all the things which they say, do not take to heart, so that you will not hear your slave cursing you!* The word order is unusual, with a long and emphatic prepositional phrase (note the emphatic *gam*) before the prohibition. In Hebrew, the phrase sounds really offbeat. It is unclear how the injunction not to take other people's words to heart would lead to Qoheleth's audience not 'hearing' their slave cursing them. It appears that Qoheleth uses the verb *šm'* with an unusual meaning, 'to be upset'. This suggests that Qoheleth is making a light-hearted comment aimed to help his audience not to take themselves too seriously when they come under fire through the things that other people say about them. The effect is comical on another count also, taking the sting out of Qoheleth's own statement in verse 20, where he had just made a strong theological claim that would have been far from flattering to his audience.

A supporting argument drives home the point, helping Qoheleth's audience reflect on their own actions: *For surely, many times over – your heart knows – you, too, have cursed others.* This argument also has an unusually odd word order and adds two further emphatic particles (*gam*). The eccentric word order and the over-the-top emphasis aim to entertain, to help Qoheleth's audience see the funny side of things when they themselves come under verbal fire.

Meaning

This part of Qoheleth's speech addresses a particularly difficult moral aspect of foreign rule in contemporary Judea: the circumstance that foreign legal values clashed with traditional Jewish beliefs in a direct relationship between deeds and their consequences, where until now justice had been enforced through a predictable and consistent legal system undergirded by shared religious values.

Qoheleth addresses a number of typical responses among the local population, such as utilitarian legalism on the one hand and cynical lawlessness on the other. At the heart of Qoheleth's endorsement of moral moderation lie verses 18–20, which extol moral decency tempered by traditional Jewish religious values, paired with a practical wisdom which promotes sociopolitical realism and a healthy dose of self-awareness.

19. REFLECTIONS ON THE RESEARCH IMPACT OF THE PRECEDING CASE STUDIES (7:23 – 8:1)

Context

Qoheleth's reflections sound like a summary statement on his intellectual enterprise of searching for success (cf. 1:3). In reality, they constitute a satirical condemnation of the foreign regime. In what sounds like a review of his 'research project' up to this point, Qoheleth reflects on the fruits of his intellectual journey. Bringing the extended send-up of the occupying force's power in 4:1 – 7:22 to a climax, he is now taking it to the next level. His at times sarcastic self-parody that initially appears self-deprecatory is in reality a verdict on the foreign empire.

Although 7:23–26 is only loosely connected with the preceding sequence, Qoheleth's reflections here form a review of his research project as a whole, as the opening phrase *All this* indicates. It refers all the way back to the beginning of Ecclesiastes 3 and perhaps even to 1:3, and concerns the entirety of Qoheleth's intellectual journey. Since Qoheleth's first case study in 1:12 – 2:26 includes a summary statement which is similar to the one here, Qoheleth may only be commenting on 3:1 – 7:22, but since the verdicts are very similar, this effectively amounts to a comment on the entire speech from its beginning.

Comment

Qoheleth's review of his 'research project' initially appears confusing, even incongruous (Krüger 2004: 143). When its ironical tone is taken into account, however, its true meaning is revealed.

23. Qoheleth introduces his review with the phrase *All this I had tested with wisdom.* Yet the next words instantly undermine this claim: *I had said: 'I want to be wise', but it remained far from me.* Despite his best efforts, the object of his inquiry not only had remained beyond his grasp, but it continued to be 'far away', a spatial reference which Qoheleth will develop shortly to hilarious effect.

The logical tension disappears when we recognize that Qoheleth is referring not to a search for wisdom, but to his pursuit of *success* (*yitrôn*), the object of his inquiry from the outset. When he claims *All this I had tested with wisdom*, then, he is referring to the entire research programme, from the beginning to the present moment. When he recalls his determination to conduct the research project with all the intellectual rigour he could muster, yet that he failed to find what he was looking for – *I had said: 'I want to be wise', but it remained far from me* – he is, then, admitting that all the wisdom he employed did not enable him to succeed in finding *success* (*yitrôn*), with the feminine personal pronoun *hî'* (*it*) referring not to wisdom (which is not the *object* of his inquiry, but the *means* he employed in his search), but to the common gender noun *yitrôn*, last mentioned in 7:12 and which has remained the object of his search all along. Qoheleth here provides a provisional, interim summary of his research findings: that his wisdom (and, by implication, anybody's wisdom) does not have the capacity to make the search for *success* (*yitrôn*) succeed. Qoheleth describes the failure of the research programme with the spatial metaphor of *it* (= *yitrôn*, success) being 'far away' from him, a metaphor for cognitive inaccessibility. This carries over into the next verse.

24. The spatial metaphor to convey incomprehensibility and cognitive malfunction continues: *What happened is far away, and deep-deep. Who can find it?* The phrase *What happened* refers to the various case studies he has undertaken or observed, not other events. In spite of the disappointing results, Qoheleth is, of course, not at all surprised, and he exploits the occasion with humorous flourish. He turns the epistemological evaluation of the experiment into an apparently embarrassed concession of defeat which blisters with self-irony, signalled through catchword repetition (*rāḥôq*, far; cf. *rĕḥôqâ*, v. 23), other spatial metaphors to complement the first, articulated in over-the-top, almost puerile fashion (*wĕʿāmōq ʿāmōq, and deep-deep*), and a defensively posed rhetorical question for an excuse. The question *Who can find it?*, no doubt exclaimed in a whining tone, is meant to suggest that nobody could possibly have discovered *what happened* (*mâ-šehāyâ*).

Qoheleth's evaluation thus ends in a rhetorical flourish that sounds pathetic, all for comic effect. Incidentally, the question also introduces a second catchword, the verb *mṣʾ*, 'to find', which recurs throughout the passage: once in verse 26, twice in verse 27, three times in verse 28 and once more in verse 29. And so Qoheleth gives his audience the opportunity to indulge in delighting over someone else's misfortune as they laugh at his expense, when in reality they laugh at themselves.

25. Qoheleth continues in a light-hearted manner. What follows is another description of his quasi-scientific approach to the cognitive challenges he faced. Similar to 1:13 the phrase *I had turned, me and my heart* signals a summary statement regarding the results which Qoheleth and his co-investigator (= his heart) had found in the extended sequence of case studies and reflections from 1:3 to 7:22. A series of three expressions then recapitulates his research method and overall approach: *to know, and to explore, and to search.* The list of activities at first glance appears to summarize Qoheleth's careful methodology. In reality, they recall the self-satirical description of the Solomonic parody's failed experiment earlier in the speech (1:13). Ultimately, this list will show in an even more pathetic light Qoheleth's failure to find what he was looking for.

The following words describe the first research objective: *wisdom and competence* (*ḥokmâ wĕḥešbôn*). The word *ḥešbôn*, the keyword in the passage, appears only three times in the Hebrew Bible (7:25, 27; 9:10; on 7:29, see below). Qoheleth here, too, is using a fashionable buzzword trending among his target audience. It is a technical or semi-technical term related to competence or professional skill which – or so his audience thought – would enable them to 'succeed', that is, to obtain *yitrôn*.

This leads to a second research objective mentioned in the verse: *and to understand wickedness, overconfidence [reša' kesel] and the irrationality, stupidity [wĕhassiklût hôlēlôt]*. The statement sounded as odd in the original Hebrew as it does in my translation. The term *reša'* refers to a well-known and common moral human quality, *wickedness*. The remaining three words, by contrast, are rare. The term *kesel* refers to *overconfidence* (cf. Ps. 78:4–6 [MT 78:5–7]; Job 8:13–15). The term *siklût* refers to *irrationality* (cf. 1:17; 2:3, 12, 13; 10:1, 13). The noun *hôlelôt* refers to *stupidity* (cf. 1:17; 2:12; 9:3; 10:13).

As Qoheleth reviews the outcome of his research programme, he is reflecting on the positive (wisdom and professional competence) and the negative (wickedness, overconfidence, irrationality and stupidity) human qualities he has encountered in himself and in the various characters that appeared throughout the programme of study. The next verse will report on the outcome of his reflections, introduced with the verb 'to find'.

26. Qoheleth presents the first item in the list of his research findings: *But I kept finding something more bitter than death*. The remainder of the verse describes what he kept finding: *the woman who – a tangle of nets she is, and a set of snares is her heart, fetters are her hands*. This comes as something of a surprise after the previous verse, which had indicated that Qoheleth was evaluating cognitive and ethical qualities. How can a dangerously captivating woman be the finding on his *cognitive* quest?

Qoheleth's reference to the dangerous woman who captivates and destroys people is based on the 'strange woman' (*'iššâ zārâ*) and the 'foreign woman' (*nokrîyâ*) of Proverbs. Qoheleth saw the danger they presented to his audience not in their sexual attraction, but in their seductive speech, which may have had nothing or little to do with sexual persuasion but rather was related to their ability to win Qoheleth's contemporaries for their cultural and religious values. Consequently, the dangerous woman whom Qoheleth has found represents the young women among the foreign elite who, through intermarriage and other social interactions with the local elites, have captivated or are threatening to captivate the hearts of unsuspecting young Jews and win them for their foreign cultural and religious values, the very things (such as, for example, the ambition to find *success*) that Qoheleth has been arguing against all along. This representative function of *the woman* whom Qoheleth has found is signalled through the direct article, which here does not signal definiteness but designates a category of woman being described. It is also signalled through the until now enigmatic participle *môṣe'*, which suggests that he kept finding this kind of woman over and over again, a realistic scenario in Qoheleth's occupied Judea.

Against this background, the remainder of verse 26 makes perfect sense: *The one who is good before God will be rescued from her, but the sinner will be captured by her.* Qoheleth is not urging his audience to refrain from intermarriage or keep away from foreign women in order to promote religious loyalty, as one might expect. Rather, he urges the young in his audience to *be good* before God, to conduct themselves in line with their God's requirements for a good life (cf. Mic. 6:8). A religiously observant life with moral integrity will save them *from her*, that is, from the corrupting influence of existing and potential foreign marriage partners. A *sinner*, by contrast, will easily yield to his wife's cultural and religious values and priorities: he *will be captured by her*. It is impossible to demonstrate that this is the only or even the best meaning of the verse. That is the point of Qoheleth's ideological camouflage. Other possible interpretations are a consequence of the underdetermined nature of Qoheleth's routine, which continues until the end of the chapter.

27–28. In verses 27–29 Qoheleth presents what appear to be two sets of further research findings. In the middle of a speech which he has been presenting for some time, he begins to report what he is saying in the form of a quotation of himself speaking as a woman: *'āmĕrâ qōhelet, says Lady Qoheleth.*[1] The third person narrative fragment

---

1. The Hebrew text is almost universally 'corrected' by transposing the letter *-h*, the third feminine singular ending on *'āmĕrâ*, to the beginning of the following word, where it becomes the definite article, resulting in *'āmar haqqōhelet*, 'says the qoheleth', as in 12:8 (see e.g. Seow 1997: 264). However, the gender switch occurs in the context of apparently

is embedded within his quotation of his own words, which introduce 'her' second research finding: *See, this is what I have found.* The phrase is repeated almost letter for letter at the beginning of verse 29, where it introduces Qoheleth's final research finding: *See, only this I have found.* The only difference between the two statements lies in the first word, *only*, and implies that whatever Qoheleth reports to have found in verses 27–28 amounts to nothing at all.

Thus, when 'Lady Qoheleth' admits, *See, only this I have found, time after time in searching for competence, which my throat [napšî] was still seeking ['ǎšer 'ôd-biqšâ], but [which] I have not found*, it is a nice touch when Qoheleth employs the third feminine singular form of the verb (*biqšâ*) describing the search of Lady Qoheleth's *throat* (*nepeš*), thus deliberately choosing that gender of the common gender noun *nepeš* which best suits his mischievous purposes. This takes on an even more comical tone considering that his throat no doubt played a particularly prominent part in his gender-bending performance as 'she' was speaking in a deliberately forced high pitch, pressing air past his constricted vocal cords (situated right next to the throat) to mimic a woman's voice. It is more than likely that Qoheleth had his audience in stitches by now.

What follows is the record of what 'Lady Qoheleth' *has* managed to find: *one man among a thousand I have found, but a woman among all of them I have not found*. Again, the two-part statement is deliberately underdetermined and ambiguous. For later readers who have failed to detect Qoheleth's humorous streak, it has sounded enigmatic and misogynist (Longman 1998: 206). Another, simpler under-standing presents itself. Since Lady Qoheleth is still looking for *ḥešbôn*, that is, success-generating competence, the first statement declares that Qoheleth has found only *one* man in a thousand men who have in fact obtained it, a devastating statistic for those who

---

misogynist statements, which indicates more than a coincidence. The frequently humorous nature of Qoheleth's speech, combined with the context, suggests that the gender switch is deliberate, aiming to amuse the audience. Further support for this conclusion comes through the apparently isolated first person singular pronoun in 8:2, which signals Qoheleth's resumption of his normal, male voice.

aim to benefit from collaborating with the foreign regime. The statement is, of course, hyperbolic and designed to help Qoheleth make his point through the words of his feminine alter ego. 'Her' high-pitched voice is then heard delivering the comic punchline, *but a woman among all of them I have not found*. More than likely, it was greeted with roaring laughter. The circumstance that this denigrating verdict on women's chances of achieving success comes from the mouth of a 'woman' adds to the hilarity.

29. 'Lady Qoheleth' now names the real and important things which she claims to have found. The sequence is packed with keyword repetitions. The verb *mṣ'* appears six times in verses 27–29. Lady Qoheleth's 'research report' uses this catchword sequence, which ostensibly lists the results of her research, to comical effect. This becomes obvious in translation: 'See, this is what I have found! – and I have not found – I have found – I have not found – see, this above all I have found!' It is as if Lady Qoheleth is all confused and flustered. After the Solomonic charade in 1:12 – 2:16, Qoheleth has now brought in a second, female alter ego in order to satirize the entire research project.

The emphasis in Lady Qoheleth's research report is on the final statement, signalled with *lĕbad*: *this alone* she found: *that God made human beings straight* [*yāšār*]; *but they have sought for many schemes* [*ḥiššĕbōnôt*]. It identifies the twisting of humans from their originally straight design into crooked specimens as a consequence of their search for extraordinary knowledge. It is a diagnostic reflection on current affairs in the light of the opening chapters of Genesis (Longman 1998: 207), equating the divine verdict that all creation, including humans, was 'very good' (Gen. 1:31) with the statement that God made humans *straight*. Consequently, the metaphor *yāšār*, *straight*, refers to intellectual *and* moral qualities (with Longman 1998: 207; contra Fox 1989: 247).

The sequence also employs an elaborate and ingenious inter-textual play on words formed from the root *ḥšb*, 'to devise, scheme' (Longman 1998: 207): the claim that humans have sought for many schemes (*ḥiššĕbōnôt*) echoes Genesis 6:5: 'The LORD saw that the wickedness of humankind was great in the earth, and that every inclination of the thoughts of their hearts was only evil continually' (NRSV). The word translated 'thoughts' is *maḥšĕbōt*, from the same root as *hiššĕbōnôt* (*schemes*) and *hešbôn* (*competence*) in Ecclesiastes. Theologically, the divine verdict on human iniquity in Genesis 6:5 is a direct consequence of the human consumption of fruit from the tree of the knowledge of good and evil in Genesis 3. Eve's discovery that the tree 'was to be desired to make one wise' (NRSV) is what Qoheleth's feminine alter ego has in mind when she makes her pronouncement *but they sought for many schemes*. The curious circumstance that in Qoheleth's own little scheme the condemnatory pronouncement on humanity's first female scheming comes from the mouth of a fellow woman is a stroke of genius. This is funny and it is meant to convict *and* entertain.

This theological statement reinterprets *hešbôn*, the success-yielding competence that Qoheleth's feminine alter ego had been searching for. Since *hešbôn* is also derived from the root *ḥšb*, and is virtually identical with the *schemes* (*hiššĕbōnôt*) that left humanity in a twist, *hešbôn* itself now appears in a new light: the success-yielding competence that many among Qoheleth's audience had themselves been searching for is now exposed for what it is: it is not a *hešbôn* at all, it is a *hiššābôn* – note the soundplay! – one of those *schemes* that led to humanity's demise in the first place and which now threatens to ruin those who would yield to the allure of foreign success.

8:1. Commonly taken to open the sequence of Ecclesiastes 8:1–9, this verse provides the hermeneutical key for Lady Qoheleth's guest appearance. The question *Who is like the wise man, and who knows how to unravel a matter?* is Lady Qoheleth's invitation to her male audience not to take her word(s) at face value, but to engage in imaginative interpretation.

The second half of the verse then furnishes a motivation for her predominantly male audience to put Qoheleth's speech, and, by implication, her own contribution to it, into perspective: *A man's wisdom lights up his face, and the stern expression on his face is softened.* Her point is that if her audience understand the hidden message in her speech, it will entertain them: to *light up* someone's face speaks of a pleasant disposition visibly communicated through facial expressions, including smiles and laughter, the physiological response which the comical design of Qoheleth's speech has aimed to inspire from the beginning. The second half of the verse, *and the stern expression on his face is softened*, promises that this way of looking at things will help those wise enough to get her hidden message to overcome depression and anger.

Meaning

Humour in the Bible is frequent and theologically significant. Much of this humour is of a dark nature. This is also true for much of the humour in Ecclesiastes. Here, however, it is both light-hearted and serious. This is an exemplar in the use of humour to communicate challenging content. It is a summary verdict on Qoheleth's search for *success*, a quest that had ended in failure and frustration. This pursuit was neither purely philosophical nor purely economic, neither purely cultural nor purely political. What was at stake was the very identity and character of Qoheleth's faith community.

20. FURTHER REFLECTIONS ON THE RESEARCH IMPACT OF THE PRECEDING CASE STUDIES (8:2–9)

Context

The following speech segment is underdetermined, saturated with ambiguity. Sounding like a loyalist admonition to obey royal commands aimed at compatriots who come into contact with high-ranking representatives of the occupying power's monarch, its ambiguous character barely conceals that in reality it is an appeal to examine foreign royal directives, to critically appraise the moral implications of such demands and to engage in passive resistance where necessary. Following the hilarious summary of Qoheleth's research agenda, Qoheleth resumes his male identity and returns to a more serious tone. He calls for measured consideration and restraint in the form of passive resistance. The language is underdetermined of necessity, for it aims to regulate human behaviour vis-à-vis a 'monarch' at the head of the occupying power.

Comment

2. The significance and function of the first word, the isolated personal pronoun *'ănî*, *I* or 'me', has eluded interpreters until now

(Murphy 1992: 80 n. 2a; Krüger 2004: 150). The circumstance that
7:23 – 8:1 was performed by Qoheleth in the high-pitched voice of
a woman had been signalled through his own narrative insertion,
says Lady Qoheleth (7:27). Consequently, the personal pronoun here
signals the end of his feminine self-caricature, helping later readers
of his speech to detect the transition even though they had never
witnessed Qoheleth's live performances. It is a stage instruction, as
it were.

Speaking in his normal voice again, Qoheleth offers the first of
two instructions. He urges his audience to carefully evaluate royal
commands: *The mouth of the king observe . . . !* Ambiguity abounds.
This is reflected in the diverse translations and interpretations in
circulation (Krüger 2004: 152–154). What does it mean to *observe*
(*šĕmôr*) the king's mouth? Initially it looks like a loyalist admonition
to obey royal commands, but the verb has been deployed subversively before (5:8). Qoheleth's audience knew exactly what he
really meant: to critically examine royal directives as to the monarch's
potentially dangerous moods and, in view of later pronouncements
in the sequence, to critically appraise the moral implications of
his demands.

During the period to which most modern scholars date the
book, there was no actual resident king. It is hard to imagine that
anyone attending Qoheleth's routine or reading his polemical
pamphlet would ever have seen the occupying power's monarch
face-to-face. Consequently, the advice is not about court etiquette;
it is guidance on how to respond to the demands of local potentates
as they enforce the absentee king's demands.

Qoheleth then presents an argument in favour of his two-faced
admonition. His audience should observe the rulers' directives
because of an oath of God. This phrase is also ambiguous. Whose oath
to whom and about what? Qoheleth's indigenous audience would
have got it straight away, but it is likely that any foreign spies in
attendance were left scratching their heads just as much as modern
interpreters. The pointlessness of the argument makes Qoheleth's
point: he only *pretends* to advocate loyalty, when in reality he subverts
it. Again, mention of the monarch triggers hyper-ambiguity.

3. Qoheleth's second instruction is ingeniously split into two
apparently independent imperatives: *Do not hurry from his presence*

when you leave, do not stand in a bad matter/word . . . ! It appears to warn the audience against leaving the king's presence, only to commend not staying in his presence in the same breath (Longman 1998: 213). The contradiction is striking, and the effect is puzzling, thought-provoking and funny. For this reason, the popular effort at sanitizing the instruction through transposing the first instruction to the end of the previous statement, thereby removing the apparent contradiction (Longman 1998: 213; Fox 1999: 277), is unnecessary.

What is more, every word apart from the negative particle in the instruction has several meanings. The adjective *rā'* can refer to something unpleasant or immoral. The noun *dābār* can mean 'word' or 'matter' or even 'situation'. The prohibition *'al-ta'ămōd* can mean 'do not delay' or 'do not stand up for'. The phrase as a whole has multiple intended meanings. Qoheleth thus can be heard to support royal authority when in fact he subverts it.

What follows are two assertions and a rhetorical question which present Qoheleth's justification for his two-faced endorsement of foreign royal authority. The first claim is true but also invites inversion: *for he can do whatever he likes.* The apparent defence of the royal prerogative can also be heard as its subversion.

4. The ambivalence continues: *For the word of a king is supreme, and who can say to him: 'What are you doing?'* On the face of it, Qoheleth again extols the royal prerogative to shore up the population's loyalty to their foreign overlords (so, e.g., Longman 1998: 212). Just beneath the surface, however, he confronts foreign political claims to absolute supremacy, and at the same time reminds his audience who their *real* king is (Krüger 2004: 154).

5. In the following, Qoheleth offers a lengthy reflection on the theological and anthropological basis for his instruction. Hyper-ambiguity prevails. First he proffers the theological basis for the recommended response to the abuse of foreign power. Obedience – to whom is not specified – will keep one out of harm's way: *He who observes a command will not know a bad word/matter.* This claim sounds and reads like a deliberate variant on earlier instructions, with a repetition of the verb *šmr* (now as a participle rather than an imperative) and the word *command* as object, which can be either the king's order or a commandment of God (Krüger 2004: 154). The consequence of obedience, Qoheleth avers, is that harm will be avoided, with the words *a bad word/matter* (wordplay!) repeated from verse 3. Again, Qoheleth invites a loyalist and a rebellious interpretation all at once.

Complementary information regarding the observance of commands follows: *and time and judgment a wise heart knows.* This also can be heard as commending obedience, or as an allusion to 3:1, 7b, 17, implying that it is *God* who is in charge of *time and judgment*, even in the realm *under the sun.*

6–7. These echoes continue and intensify: *because for every matter there is the proper time and judgment, because the evil of human beings is large upon them, because they cannot know what will be, because who can tell them how it will turn out?* These statements form a string of four justifications. They can be heard and read both as a series of general observations on the vagaries of life (Longman 1998: 213–214) and as a critique of the foreign royal prerogative expressed earlier (Krüger 2004: 156).

8. Now Qoheleth turns to present the anthropological basis for his instruction on the proper response to the abuse of royal power. A series of five negations can and should be read as a devastating critique of foreign royal claims to supremacy: *There is no human being who can exert supremacy over the wind, [no-one] who can restrain the wind, no-one who can be supreme over the day of death and no-one who can gain release from military service during the battle; and neither can wickedness rescue its master.*

There is a double meaning, with the two mentions of the word *rûaḥ* simultaneously suggesting the meanings 'wind' and 'spirit'. While Qoheleth wants the meaning 'wind' to be in the foreground for the sake of plausible deniability, the background meaning reminds his audience that even the foreign king cannot ultimately overpower the inner world of the human spirit. This is also insinuated in barely hidden fashion through the mention of two words formed from the root *šlṭ*, which had referred to the supremacy of the foreign king's command just a moment earlier (v. 4). Yet if no human being can control the wind (or the human spirit), how can the king, for all his military might?

The remainder of the verse continues in comedian-style doublespeak. While the next line appears to affirm military discipline (no-one can obtain release from military service when the enemy is engaged), the final line, clearly the climax of the sequence and Qoheleth's punchline, appears to affirm ultimate royal control and at the same time sarcastically exposes the king as the ultimate 'master of wickedness', who himself will not be able to escape the consequence of his evil actions.

9. Qoheleth rounds off his instructions on how to respond to the abuse of royal power, and places his critique of foreign rule into a social and ethical perspective. The verse describes the socio-political circumstances that had prompted his reflection on the abuse of power, which had led to the series of instructions in this part of the routine.

The opening phrase serves as an introduction similar to earlier ones (see esp. 1:14): *All this I saw.* In company with the particle *all*, the demonstrative pronoun refers back to a longer range of observations, which at a minimum includes the material in 8:2–8, more likely the larger material from 7:25 to 8:8, and possibly all the material in his speech, from 1:4 right up to this point. The next phrase, *as I dedicated my heart to all deeds that are done under the sun*, indicates a serious intellectual inquiry into the foreign regime's policies and their impact on local life. The final part of the verse provides a temporal reference in apposition to the activities unfolding under the sun: *a time when the man exerts supremacy over another man to his detriment.* As often is the case, the direct article in *hā'ādām* can either indicate the category of human beings in general, or it can refer to a specific human being, such as the foreign king or the highest foreign official ruling the land. Qoheleth designed ambiguity into much of his speech. This is true also for the next words: *to his detriment* can designate negative consequences either for the one ruled or for the ruler himself. Either way, Qoheleth ends daringly with an only thinly veiled critique of the negative impact that the foreign rule has exerted on his community, the kinds of problems that prompted the series of coping strategies he has presented in 8:2–8.

Meaning
This speech segment addresses a specific sociopolitical situation in the life of post-exilic Judea, a period when the country had been reduced to a province by a foreign power with soldiers' feet on the

ground. It urges the local population to measured but determined passive resistance and perhaps even civil disobedience in cases where the foreign demands clash with the religiously motivated values and ethical standards of the local population.

21. FURTHER REFLECTIONS ON THE ABUSE OF POWER (8:10–14)

Context

After an instruction on passive resistance or civil disobedience (8:2–9), Qoheleth now recounts a particularly explosive situation that had recently occurred. The description of his own fury and resentment represents the emotional response of the population as a whole, and epitomizes the kinds of situations that necessitate the forms of passive resistance which he has just advocated. Due to the explosive nature of the situation, much here is deliberately underdetermined.

Comment

10. After a transitional phrase which hints at continuity with the previous observations – *And in that same context* – Qoheleth describes a scene that disturbed and offended him: *I saw the wicked being buried.* It is not the funeral itself that has raised his concerns, but the events that had led up to the burial ceremony. While he observed the funeral ceremony itself with his physical eyes, he also considered three events that had happened earlier, events that were connected with problematic actions related to a visit to a religious site consecrated for worship: *And they had come, and they had gone from a holy place.* What the circumstances of this visit were, we are not told. What is implied, however, is that what they had done there was improper. And, considering the explosive nature of what had occurred, Qoheleth's audience would have known exactly what specific event he was talking about.

The phrase *and they were forgotten in the city* is preserved in many Hebrew manuscripts with a variant spelling. Substituting one similar letter in the verb, they have turned the word into a different verb with the meaning 'and they boasted'. In this variant, the statement highlights that the people who were being buried had not only done something improper, but they had subsequently boasted publicly about it.

Every word in the four descriptions is transparent, and the grammar and syntax of the verse as a whole is unproblematic. Why is it, then, that the verse is considered the most difficult in the book (Krüger 2004: 159; Longman 1998: 218)?

The answer is this: numerous items in this brief scene are *deliberately underdetermined.* Qoheleth is alluding to a recent incident that had offended religious Jewish sensitivities. Foreigners had desecrated a religious site, probably the temple in Jerusalem. It appears that the offence had led to violent retaliation, causing the deaths of at least some of the foreign offenders, who were now being buried, no doubt with military pomp and honours. It is reasonable to assume that many more Jews were killed subsequently by the foreign regime. Qoheleth is disgusted by the disconnect between the high honours extended to the bodies of the foreign perpetrators and their despicable acts while they were still alive. In the highly sensitive and explosive situation, however, Qoheleth keeps his comments so vague that only insiders would have known what he was talking about. The words were clear; their referents were not. This is the ingenuity of the ideological dissenter, who dares to raise his voice against foreign control but hides behind plausible deniability.

Qoheleth now offers an extended evaluation of this instance, beginning with the refrain-like statement we have encountered throughout his speech: *This really is a mirage!* The scene he has observed appears to reflect as normal that people who have committed serious crimes (such as violating the Jewish temple in Jerusalem) can get away with it under foreign rule. This has created a mirage, the false impression that actions do not have consequences.

11. A generalization drawn from the scene highlights that delayed punishment encourages further abuse: *When a sentence is not executed quickly against a crime, then human hearts are filled within them to do what is wrong.* The claim is deliberately vague as to whether such delay results from divine or human causes, or both. While this circumstance veils Qoheleth's critique of foreign rule (plausible deniability), those in the know would nonetheless quickly pick up that he was referring to the favouritism of the foreign judicial system when it came to their own, as described in verse 10.

12. The real problem with this mirage is theological. Qoheleth describes the cause of the illusion – the circumstance that serious criminals who serially offend sometimes live long lives: *when a sinner does evil things a hundred times but lives a long life.* There appears to be a tension with the funeral scene, which implies that some people had died for their offences. However, their deaths appear to have resulted from mob justice, not from divine retribution or punishment under the law. Very likely, several other offenders escaped the mob, and were now prominent among the mourners.

What follows explains the theological reality obscured by the illusion, beginning with Qoheleth's claim to certainty: *because I also know.* Then comes the confirmation that retribution will indeed happen – there will be an eventual reward for God-fearers: *that it will turn out well for those who fear God,* with the phrase *when they fear from before him* referring to a continual God-fearing lifestyle before God.

13. Conversely, there will also be an eventual retribution for the wicked: *and it will not turn out well for the wicked, and his days will not lengthen like a shadow, because he has not walked in fear before God.* These statements form the theological core of the segment.

14. Usually, this is taken to be yet another perturbed and disillusioned outcry expressing general frustration with life (Longman 1998: 220–221): *It is a mirage that takes place on earth!* Two circumstances suggest an alternative. (1) The mirage statement forms an inclusio with a similar statement at the beginning of the segment (*This really is a mirage*, v. 10). (2) Therefore, the mirage which Qoheleth describes here consists of the events to which he refers in verse 10, the actual events that have unfolded before his eyes in the original inflammatory incident, the resultant bloody skirmishes and finally the funeral, which quite literally are *the case when the righteous are treated as if they had acted like the wicked, and the case when wicked people are treated as if they had acted like the righteous.*

In the end, Qoheleth is so frustrated with the foreign regime's mishandling of the affair that he cannot help but repeat the verdict for a third time: *This really is, I say, a mirage!* His point is not that the lack of imminent retributive justice renders life meaningless. Rather, he declares the lack of imminent retributive justice witnessed here and elsewhere in human experience to be an illusion. In the end, all will receive from God what they deserve, as he has already affirmed in verses 12b–13, the theological heart of the sequence.

Meaning

This segment of Qoheleth's speech sequence arises from a specific incident of injustice and evil as a consequence of the political situation of his time, but the problem of politically sanctioned injustice and persistent evil is universal and timeless. It poses fundamental anthropological questions about human nature on the one hand, and serious questions about the goodness of God, the problem of theodicy in classical philosophy, on the other.

Qoheleth introduces the *dynamic of time* into the debate. The theological centrepiece of his reflection then affirms that God will *eventually* reward believers who act morally and will punish those who refused to believe and refused to act in accordance with the divine will. Partial reward and punishment may or may not occur in this earthly life. They certainly will happen in the life that is to come.

22. CONCLUDING REFLECTIONS ON THE ABUSE OF POWER AND THE APPARENT INCONGRUITY BETWEEN DEEDS AND THEIR CONSEQUENCES (8:15 – 9:1)

Context

Qoheleth wrestles with the theological problem that it is their own God who has imposed the challenging sociopolitical circumstances under foreign rule upon his people. After the theological anchor in 8:10–14, Qoheleth now draws practical conclusions, commending in his fifth *carpe diem* statement the active enjoyment of life, irrespective of sociopolitical circumstances.

Comment

15. This verse may also conclude the preceding segment; the transitions from one part to another in this long speech are often fluid. Qoheleth now draws practical conclusions from the distressing circumstances of pervasive injustice he has just described. In connection with 8:14, Longman interprets Qoheleth's commendation of joy negatively (Longman 1998: 221). Others take it more positively (Whybray 1982; Krüger 2004: 162). The commendations to enjoy life are defiant coping mechanisms for overcoming despondency. After all, it is God who has brought about the depressing circumstances under foreign rule.

16. This leads to a brief but intense reflection in verses 16–17 and 9:1 on the complexity of the cognitive task which Qoheleth and his audience are facing, enclosed between two complementary phrases: *When I gave my heart to know wisdom* (8:16) and *For all this I gave to my heart* (9:1). This frame highlights that Qoheleth invests considerable cognitive energy in the curious and thus amusing discoveries in 8:16–17: *the business which is done on earth* is apparently an undertaking that leads to universal insomnia: *even that there is no-one who sees sleep with his eyes by day or by night.* Hyperbole (universal insomnia) and incongruence (when people sleep, their eyes are typically closed, so they cannot see anything, let alone see sleep) combine to create comic relief. The phrase is perhaps a dig at the restless striving and the insatiable desire for more of those who have adopted the value system of the foreign regime (cf. 2:10; 4:8; 11:9).

17. Qoheleth's considerations then lead into the report on a new insight: *then I saw the full extent of God's doing.* This hyperbolical assertion *pretends* to claim comprehensive understanding of the divine work *while in the same breath* denying that such insight is possible: *that the man cannot find out all doing that is done under the sun!* The intentional contradiction is amusing and entertaining. No amount of intellectual effort will yield the desired results: *however hard he works to search it out, he cannot find it!* Even the wise, those with a reputation for cognitive excellence, cannot grasp it.

The crucial component for identifying the sphere of human ignorance is the key phrase *under the sun*, which here, too, serves as the cypher for foreign rule over Judea. Poignantly, he also affirms that this sociopolitical status quo is imposed by God, and he admits that this divine move remains incomprehensible.

9:1. This understanding of the segment finds support in the highly ambiguous words which follow and round off the portion: *For all this I gave to my heart in order to examine it all.* The repeated demonstrative pronoun in combination with the word *all* indicates that Qoheleth is referring to the complex sociopolitical situation as a whole. Qoheleth talks as if the cognitive challenge of working out the proper response to the sociopolitical problems was too much for him, forcing him to pass on the matter to a cognitive sidekick, his heart. Despite the serious subject matter, the effect is probably meant to be comical.

The next words express the outcome of his heart's contemplation: *how the righteous and the wise and their activities are in the hand of God – also love, also hatred.* Very likely following a pause for dramatic effect, this outburst (its intensity is expressed through the introductory relative pronoun) reminds Qoheleth's community that the success of their responses to the sociopolitical circumstances depends on God alone.

The two nouns *love* and *hatred* may belong with the preceding or the following words. The text is ambiguous. It is not clear who the subjects or the objects of these verbal nouns are. It seems the author wanted to be intentionally opaque (cf. 3:1–8). In the light of the subversive nature of Qoheleth's rhetoric throughout, it is therefore likely that here, too, he is referring to his community's resistance efforts against wholesale Hellenization. The success of whatever resistance Qoheleth's community will be able to muster remains uncertain: *the man does not know anything that is before them*, that is, they do not even know whether their efforts will be rewarded with admiration and respect (= *love*) or scorn and disdain (= *hate*) from their own community, or even from God.

Meaning

Qoheleth's approach is intellectually honest and theologically realistic, and his admission of ignorance indicates humility and courage. He refuses to offer simple solutions to the theological and intellectual conundrum that the Jewish God had permitted foreign rule to persist into his time, and he also admits that ultimately neither he nor his community know what to do under the circumstances. Modern Christian and Jewish preaching in the face of similarly complex issues may find a helpful role model in Qoheleth's modesty.

23. REFLECTION ON THE UNIVERSALITY OF DEATH, IRRESPECTIVE OF MORAL OR RELIGIOUS QUALITIES (9:2–10)

Context

This segment explores implications from the moral conundrum of universal human mortality, irrespective of merit. Qoheleth urges his audience to rediscover the true sources of happiness which the traditional values and aspirations of Jewish faith provide. Following directly after Qoheleth's commendation of active enjoyment (8:15 – 9:1), this segment highlights that in an uncertain world whose political parameters the members of his audience cannot escape, they can find purpose and satisfaction in those areas of their lives which they can control.

Comment

2. Qoheleth claims an identical fate for all human beings, irrespective of ethical or religious qualities. What that common fate is will only be revealed at the end of verse 3, building suspense. The phrase *Everything is the same for everybody* is hyperbolical, for rhetorical effect, as only one commonality is in view. Four groups of persons with contrasting qualities are being compared. The enumeration is not designed to present a comprehensive list of precise qualities; rather, Qoheleth lists them for rhetorical effect, because they are representative of all human beings, no matter their moral, religious or intellectual qualities or actions. The fate of *all* is the same, no matter who or what they are or how they conduct their lives.

3. This verse exposes the extent to which *evil* has penetrated all human activity on earth, especially in the current climate under foreign occupation (*in all that is done under the sun*, specifically mentioning the cypher for foreign rule). The phrase *that/for there is one fate for all* prompts Qoheleth's inquiry into the nature and extent of human evil, for the apparent incongruence between a universally negative outcome despite moral and religious differences between human beings is itself a moral conundrum.

The remainder of the verse shows that the commonality of death is not itself evil, but is evil's most prominent consequence. As in 7:29 and 8:6, Qoheleth here alludes to the early chapters of the book of Genesis, especially Genesis 6:5 (cf. Gen. 8:21). Qoheleth's therapeutic achievement is that he takes seriously the conundrum created by the circumstance that all human beings must die, irrespective of merit. His theological achievement is that he exposes that common destiny as the natural consequence of divine judgment on human wickedness, in line with Genesis 3:16–17 (Krüger 2004).

4–5a. In verses 4–10 Qoheleth draws practical conclusions. He paints a sharp contrast between the living and the dead, emphasizing the positive opportunities that life affords and highlighting the finality of death and its dire consequences. He concludes the sequence with four instructions on how his audience can make the best of life while they can.

The living have three advantages over the dead. First, in verse 4 Qoheleth strongly affirms that the living have ground for hope (*biṭṭāḥôn*; cf. 2 Kgs 18:19; Isa. 36:4). The statement is unusual. Following the *ketib*, the Hebrew seems to be composed as a question followed by its answer: *who [is the one] who should be chosen? – With all the living, there is hope.* Qoheleth's audience should choose to be among the living rather than give up on life prematurely or provoke retaliation from the foreign regime with foolhardy and rebellious talk or conduct.

He reinforces this with a sarcastic proverb, which provides his second advantage for the living over the dead: *As for a living dog: it is better off than a dead lion!* Many consider the proverb to be bitterly self-ironic, undermining the very thing it appears to promote (Longman 1998: 228). However, the opposite is true (Krüger 2004: 170). Negative attitudes towards canines and the associated sarcastic irony of the proverb strengthen rather than weaken Qoheleth's point.

His third reason for postulating an advantage for the living over the dead lies in the circumstance that *the living know that they will die* (v. 5a). Scholarly opinions about this apparent advantage are divided. Longman, for example, notes: 'That advantage is, simply, consciousness' (Longman 1998: 228). By contrast, Krüger, quoting from Lohfink, argues that 'it is not the driving out or playing down of death, but only the consciousness of having to die, that "enables one to live properly. One can take hold of joy as the God-given lot in life, then, when occasion arises, take powerful action"' (Krüger 2004: 170; Lohfink 2003). The underdetermined nature of Qoheleth's speech allows multiple interpretations.

5b–6. Five circumstances demonstrate the pitiable state of the dead and promote the benefits of being alive. First, they lack consciousness; second, there is no further reward for them; third, nobody will remember them; fourth, their emotions have perished with them; fifth, the influence of the dead upon the world of the living is denied: *and they will never again have a share in anything that is done under the sun.* The final claim, with its cypher for the oppressive foreign regime, can and should also be heard in its sociopolitical context: once dead, there is nothing that they can contribute to the indigenous population's resistance efforts. Here, too, Qoheleth relies on the occupying foreigners' incapacity to understand the finer nuances of his coded talk.

7. In verses 7–10 Qoheleth addresses his audience directly with admonitions phrased as imperatives. By some distance the highest concentration of verb forms with imperative force (seven in four verses) in Qoheleth's speech, this signals that what Qoheleth recommends here is central to the message he aims to bring across in the speech as a whole.

In verse 7, the beginning of the sixth *carpe diem* passage, the opening appeal *Go* intensifies the urgency with which Qoheleth commends the following actions, to eat with joy and drink *with a good heart*, a multivalent phrase which can mean both 'with a glad heart' and 'with good understanding', that is, in moderation and thus 'with a good conscience'. The recommended manner of consumption and the pursuit of happiness is lavish and vigorous, but not self-centred and egotistical, as in the Solomonic caricature. It is a manner of pursuing happiness which God condones, *for God has already approved what you do!* This is a commendation of a life lived well, embracing the simple but good things in life (such as food and drink) as gifts from a generous God.

8. The appeal to seize the day continues in exuberant idiom: *At all times let your clothes be white and do not let oil be lacking on your head!* These are more than the 'bare necessities of life', but they are not items of conspicuous luxury either. They are the ordinary good things in life, relatively modest pleasures such as festive clothing and oil used for skin care, items that were 'relatively easily available', as the phrase *At all times* suggests (Krüger 2004: 171–172).

9. Qoheleth recommends the pleasures of married life. In the context of his traditional society and in contrast with Greek and modern Western culture, the commendation that one should do this *with a woman whom you love* suggests that a spouse whom one loves is a prerequisite for accomplishing this feat.

The next three phrases describe the difficult sociopolitical circumstances of life under foreign rule. The density of these descriptions complicates their interpretation. (1) The phrase *which he has given to you under the sun* signals that it is God (last mentioned in v. 7) who has fabricated the pressing conditions under foreign rule. The implication is that Qoheleth's audience can do nothing to escape them. (2) The repeated mention of the word *all* (*all the days of the life of your mirage . . . all the days of your mirage*) signals lifelong commitment to one's marriage partner as a second prerequisite for happiness (Krüger 2004: 172). (3) The repeated mention of *heblekā, your mirage*, signals that Qoheleth's audience have already bought into or are already very attracted to the illusory outlook on life promoted by the foreign elite. They have made the mirage their own, and this is the development that Qoheleth has sought to reverse or prevent all along.

True happiness, Qoheleth implies, can be achieved only through the traditional Jewish values of family life. Moreover, for family life to flourish and endure, Qoheleth's audience will have to abandon their new value system (*your mirage*), an undertaking that will not come easily. Thus, the remainder of the verse provides a motivational clause: *for that is your share in this life.* The promise of Qoheleth's life-coaching programme may be a moderate one (a *ḥeleq*, *share*, that is, a partial success rather than a *yitrôn*, success), but at least it is realistic, something that can be achieved in the here and now (*baḥayyim*, *in this life*), not like the doomed hope for success in a life beyond (*biš'ôl*), as verse 10 will go on to say.

Qoheleth's scheme is also realistic in its assessment of the amount of determination and effort that will be required in order to overcome the attractive alternative ideology promoted by the foreign regime, with its allure of power and the promise of happiness through affluence.

10. It is for this reason that a climactic instruction urges commitment and vigorous action: *Everything your hand finds to do, do with your might.* There is disagreement on the meaning of the imperative in conjunction with what Qoheleth's audience find for their hand to do. Some think it is a 'complete licence to do whatever one can and wants'. Others propose that it is a call to hard work. Longman suggests that it may be both (Longman 1998: 231). The larger context suggests that the phrase *Everything your hand finds to do* relates to the life-affirming conduct which Qoheleth has just recommended.

Meaning

This segment is one of the most provocative and engaging in Qoheleth's speech. Its evocative topic and formulation, paired with its tantalizingly underdetermined multivalence, invites its audience to embark on an adventure of the mind. What does it mean to be alive? What are the important things in life?

Memento mori ('remember you will die'), the adage so popular among medieval Christians, encapsulates the foundation for Qoheleth's invitation to live life to the full. The inevitability of death stimulates a more conscious, intentional way of life, and a propensity for joy and gratitude.

24. REFLECTION ON THE PRECARIOUS UNPREDICTABILITY OF HUMAN LIFE (9:11–12)

Context

This segment flows directly from the preceding reflection. It highlights the dangerous unpredictability of human life. The experience of pervasive unfairness which Qoheleth's community continues to face is a direct consequence of adversarial external forces – a covert dig at the foreign regime.

Comment

11. There is virtual unanimity among interpreters that here Qoheleth refers to human life in general (Fox 1999: 295; Longman 1998: 232). However, the focus is on the precarious unpredictability of Jewish life under foreign rule. This is signalled through the opening phrase, which uses familiar vocabulary (cf. 4:1) in its own unique style: *I turned and saw under the sun.* The familiar cypher for foreign rule, especially prominent here, indicates that it is the arbitrary behaviour of the foreign regime that undercuts the normal rules of life. It is *under the sun* that *the race is not to the swift, nor the battle to the heroes* [note the martial idiom], *nor bread to the wise, nor wealth to the insightful, nor favour to the knowledgeable.* Frictions arising from the sociopolitical climate are in fact audible in the choice of Qoheleth's examples: competition (the swift do not win the race), mortal combat (heroes lose the battle), social standing (knowledge does not win popularity).

Plausible deniability notwithstanding, it is likely that the capricious behaviour of the foreign elite often led to unpredictable outcomes, no matter what kind and level of skill the indigenous population was able to muster, and this is what Qoheleth complains about, verbalizing the population's frustration.

Next comes the first of two rationales for Qoheleth's observations: *for time and chance happen to them all*, referring to the erratic behaviour of the foreign rulers, which undercuts the normal rules of public life through favouritism of those friendly to their interests.

12. Here is Qoheleth's second rationale: *For indeed, human beings do not know their time.* This does not refer to death in general, despite the virtual unanimity among commentators. Rather, it refers to the moment when any given Jew comes into conflict with foreign interests. This is *their time*, the moment when misfortune suddenly befalls them.

And so Qoheleth compares them to fish and birds. Although the foreign occupiers are not mentioned explicitly, the first of the two comparisons alludes to their role as 'fishers of men' through the at first sight odd addition of the word *evil* to qualify the extremely rare and unusual noun *mĕṣôdâ*, *net*. The nets of ordinary fishermen are not usually considered immoral, but it is, of course, not ordinary fishermen that Qoheleth is talking about.

Some comment on the noun *mĕṣôdâ*, *net*, is in order, especially in view of the appearance of the homonym *mĕṣôdîm*, *siege works*, in the next sequence of Qoheleth's routine, which also refers to hostile foreign interference in Jewish life. The word *mĕṣôdâ* appears only three times in the Old Testament, here and in the contested attestations in Isaiah 29:7 and Ezekiel 19:9. Why did Qoheleth choose such a rare word when there were perfectly suitable alternatives readily available?[1] As we shall see, he is preparing the way for an ingenious pun with the word *mĕṣôdîm* in verse 14.

---

1. The most common word for 'net' is *rešet*, which frequently appears in Job and Proverbs.

The final part of verse 12 expands the comparison: *like them, so human beings are snared at an evil time, when it suddenly falls upon them.* Here the *evil time* is identified with the *evil net* in the first comparison, and it does not necessarily refer to the time of one's death (so virtually all commentators), but to a serious conflict of interests with the occupying power, which may, of course, have a deadly outcome, as the metaphoric images of net and snare earlier in the verse suggest. The theme of military hostilities, only hinted at here, is tackled more directly in the next sequence.

Meaning

Homo lupus homini ('man is wolf to man'). This famous Latin proverb, which likens human beings who hold power over others to the wolf, one of the predators at the top of the food chain in the animal world, encapsulates what Qoheleth is getting at here. Greed is *not* good, and whenever one part of the human population seek their own advantage at the expense of others, the normal rules of public life no longer apply. The solution to the problem of evil and human suffering in the world begins with a religious move: large-scale repentance of the human race as a whole for what we have been and still are doing to each other. Next, such repentance must lead to a new set of values and behaviours, inspired by the love of God and neighbour, and energized by the Holy Spirit.

25. CASE STUDY 10: WISDOM WITHOUT WEALTH IGNORED (9:13 – 10:4)

Context

A miniature type-scene describing how the advice of a poor wise man who could have saved his community was ignored because of his low economic status serves as an allegory to guide the internal debates about the politics of the day. Pronouncements in the form of six traditional proverbs and a concluding exhortation present Qoheleth's advice on how to conduct the internal political dialogue wisely and successfully. The example of *wisdom* which follows has played itself out *under the sun*, under foreign rule. The scene is significant for Qoheleth's audience, and the advice he is about to give relates to internal debates among Jews on how to interact wisely with the foreign regime.

Comment

13. The introduction to Qoheleth's tenth case study is brief but packed with content. In just nine words, he provides a transitional introduction, a thematic categorization, and emphasizes its significance: *I also saw this [example of] wisdom under the sun, and it is great to me.*

The word *also* links what follows with 9:11–12. This example of wisdom takes place under foreign rule, as the cypher *under the sun* indicates. Qoheleth signals that the miniature scene he is about to describe is more relevant and significant than his laconic description suggests.

14. A type-scene describes the exemplary wisdom under scrutiny. First comes the situational brief: *A small city with few men in it, and a great king came against it, surrounded it and built siege works against it.* The art of compression on display here is masterful, drawing a vivid and complex word scene before the eyes of his audience's imagination with few words. His artful play on contrasts captures the imagination: a *small* city with *few* men in it; a *great* king building *great* siege works against it.

The Hebrew for *siege works* reads a plural form of the word *māṣôd*. The word was chosen to echo its homonym *mĕṣôdâ, net*, in 9:12 and in 7:26. Qoheleth is having fun with this pun, and it has a regime-critical punch. An emendation to *mĕṣûrîm* (also with the meaning *siege works*), in two Hebrew manuscripts whose copyists missed the joke, would spoil the fun.

15. An interesting and unusual protagonist who had the capacity to change the dynamics is introduced into the scene: *and a poor wise man was found in it, and he was the one who [could have] delivered the city through his wisdom, but nobody paid attention to that poor man.* The miniature scene is underdetermined, as the lively and unresolved debates among scholars demonstrate (Ringgren and Zimmerli 1981; Murphy 1992: 97; Longman 1998: 234; Fox 1999: 299; Krüger 2004: 176, 179).

Was Qoheleth talking about an actual event that happened recently? What was the name of the small city? Who was the great king? Who was the poor wise man? And how could he have saved the city, or how did he save the city? It is impossible for later readers to answer these questions with certainty. Qoheleth's audience, however, might have ventured a few informed guesses.

Yet a precise identification of the referents in the miniature scene is not at all necessary for the point Qoheleth is making: if only the city had listened to the man, irrespective of his material status! Ultimately, Qoheleth is coaxing his audience into paying attention to the wisdom *he* is presenting to them, a wisdom that has the capacity to save them from their own sociopolitical dilemma. He is talking about the next sequence in his routine.

16. A brief introduction (*And I said*) signals that Qoheleth is launching into a soliloquy, embedded in his speech, to present his audience with a record of his internal thought process in response to the scenario he has just described. He presents his soliloquy as a hoard of *conventional* wisdom, not as a series of new insights of his own.

Qoheleth provides an explanation for the phenomenon that wisdom without wealth tends to be ignored: *wisdom is better than heroism, but the wisdom of the poor is despised.* The next phrase may also belong to the proverb, but it is more likely that it represents Qoheleth's frustrated conclusion from the facts just stated: *and his words are not heard.* The key interpretive issue in this proverbial pronouncement is the determination of its function in context. The critical potential of the saying challenges Qoheleth's audience to go against the trend and heed true wisdom when they hear it, irrespective of the source's economic and social status.

17. Qoheleth presents a second proverb: *The words of the wise in calm are heard, more than the shouting of a ruler among fools.* The reference to *calm* is ambiguous. The words of the wise may be heard because they are spoken calmly, or because they are listened to calmly (Murphy 1992: 97). Ambiguity is Qoheleth's weapon of choice throughout his speech, so both interpretations are intended. Similar ambiguity pertains to the words *môšel bakkĕsîlîm.* This can mean a 'ruler among fools' (Longman 1998: 236), or it can be connected with the expression *nišmā'îm*, 'rulers are heard among fools' (Fox 1999: 300). The ambiguity adds interest and intrigue. The aggressive, loud-mouthed assertions of leaders will always find a lot of followers among fools. The proverb encourages Qoheleth's hearers to resist the temptation and to be wise instead.

18. In the next five verses (9:18 – 10:4), Qoheleth presents his solution for overcoming disregard for wisdom without wealth. To this end, he fires off another four proverbial sayings, capped with a practical instruction.

The proverb in verse 18 develops the point that recognition of wisdom's merit and efficacy is dependent on the audience's own wise discernment: *Wisdom is better than instruments of war, but one sinner/bungler can destroy much good.* Qoheleth continues to endorse the importance of wisdom for dealing with the current crisis: if his audience employ wisdom, they have the capacity to prevail against the might of empire, even its weapons of war. But they cannot afford to make mistakes, for just one bungler can undo all that their communal wisdom has achieved, and inflict much harm.

10:1. Wisdom is easily undone. Qoheleth launches a quirkily funny proverb to ridicule would-be offenders against the wisdom he prescribes. It is an implicit comparison: just as *Dead flies cause fine perfume to smell and bubble*, so *a little folly weighs more than wisdom, more than honour*. The sarcasm is biting, funny and effective, for who would want to be one of those *dead flies* that spoil the aroma of the community's fight for survival under foreign rule? The proverb urges Qoheleth's audience to caution, vigilance and self-control. They must not behave in ways that invite retaliation or expose the passive–aggressive strategy of wise resistance which Qoheleth counsels. Despite its passive nature, there is *honour* (*kābôd*) in what he proposes. Yet even a little folly, such as violent retaliation prompted by youthful pride, will undo it all. There is a wordplay on *weight* (*yāqār*) and *honour* (*kābôd*), which literally means 'heaviness' (Latin *gravitas*), a metaphor for honour.

2. It is against this dire warning that Qoheleth offers another funny proverb about folly: *The heart of the wise to his right, the heart of the fool to his left*. The saying is constricted to an unusual degree, even for a proverb, and its concision prompts the imagination to produce a wide range of meanings. Is it about 'good luck' ('to the right') versus 'misfortune' ('to the left') (Krüger 2004: 180)? Or is it about right and wrong and the presence and absence of power (Ogden 1987: 165)? Or should the verse not rather be read as a joke, in conjunction with verse 3, where the heart of the fool is said to be absent (Fox 1999: 302)?

3. The final specimen in this string of proverbs highlights the incorrigibility of fools: *And even when the fool walks on the road, his heart is absent and tells everyone: he is a fool*. The opening expression *And even* signals that Qoheleth's proverbial string is reaching its hilarious climax. The proverb gains its comical energy from the combination of three deliberate ambiguities.

First, there is a double meaning: the phrase *libbô ḥāser* can either mean that the fool lacks sense or it can be taken literally – that is, since the heart has wandered off to the fool's left (v. 2), as it were, it is now absent and he lacks the capacity to think straight (Fox 1999: 302). Second, the verb 'and [he/it] tells' can have either the fool or his heart as subject, with hilarious consequences. Third, the phrase *he is a fool* can have two meanings, because the referent of the personal pronoun is ambiguous: it can be either the fool himself, or everyone else (*lakkōl*) whom he meets on the road. Every constellation of these variables leads to side-splitting consequences.

4. With his audience probably still in stitches, Qoheleth moves in for the kill, presenting the lesson he wants his audience to adopt above all else: *If the spirit of the ruler rises against you*, he counsels, *do not forsake your position, for calmness can calm great offences.* Every part of this instruction is hyper-ambiguous (Krüger 2004: 219). It can be heard as encouraging opportunism. It can also be heard as a critique of opportunism. And it can be heard as a call to engage in civil disobedience.

Meaning
Qoheleth's type-scene has a universal and timeless quality. Sadly, it describes a constant in public human discourse: that a person's capacity to shape public opinion is largely determined by his or her economic status.

Qoheleth's solution for a society to acquire wisdom and discernment in and through public discourse and political debate still rings true today. True wisdom deserves attention, irrespective of the source's economic and social status. Civil discourse is essential for successful public debate. The recognition of wisdom's merit in public discourse is dependent upon the wisdom of all members of a society. General education of the population is necessary but not sufficient; the flourishing of human communities depends on more than the acquisition of knowledge. For this reason, the humanities are essential to public education and therefore need to be funded and promoted accordingly. Moderation and self-control are essential for successful public discourse, but it also needs a dose of humour, as Qoheleth's quirkily funny proverbs illustrate.

26. CASE STUDY 11: ERRORS AND RISKS IN DAILY LABOUR (10:5–15)

Context

Taken in isolation, this segment is underdetermined to the point of obscurity. When interpreted against the background of incompetent foreign governance, it makes a powerful point for Qoheleth's intended audience, while its regime-critical impact would have been lost on the governing authorities.

The segment relates to a particularly irksome policy introduced by the foreign regime: their subversive programme of promoting low-life Jewish collaborators at the expense of the Jewish elite.

Comment

5. Serious flaws in the foreign regime's conduct are in focus. What Qoheleth observes is a moral *evil* (*rā'â*), and it happens *under the sun*, Qoheleth's cypher for foreign rule. The second half of the verse assigns blame: the problematic situation results from an error of judgment at or near the centre of power. The title *šallîṭ* is Qoheleth's favourite designation for the foreign overlords and/or their ruler (Lohfink 1981) (cf. 7:19; 8:8). The unusual phrase *that* *comes out from the presence of the sovereign*, as awkward in Hebrew as it is in English, indicates that the directive originated from the sovereign and his inner circle. The rare word *šĕgāgâ* usually describes an inadvertent sin or an unintentional mistake. Qoheleth draws a comparison between this particular incident and the Jewish concept of inadvertent sins, which suggests that, whatever directive or decision had been issued, it resulted in problematic yet unintended side effects rather than wilful harm, a claim which nonetheless is peppered with irony.

6–7. A description of the consequences of the foreign administration's policy follows. The counter-intuitive contrast between *folly* and the *rich* (rather than 'wise people') is often seen to expose an 'aristocratic mind-set' (Lauha 1978) and an interest in protecting 'the advantages of privilege' (Crenshaw 2005). Such notions are anachronistic. Rather, this contrast is regime-critical and funny, for in an ancient mindset, the idea of foolish people occupying positions of highest dignity when the wise were reduced to second place would have been considered incongruous and highly unlikely, while the idea of the rich and the aristocracy walking on foot alongside slaves on horseback would have seemed outright ridiculous and crazy. This kind of role reversal, made possible through the foreign regime's policies to undermine the indigenous elite and promote loyalty among their former servants, the nouveau-riche collaborators who have benefited from their former masters' downfall, would have seemed incomprehensible and *evil* indeed. The next verses subversively highlight the dangers associated with this kind of destabilizing social experiment.

8–9. A quick-fire proverbial string in these verses appears to describe risks associated with manual labour. The list is frequently seen to 'illustrate the uncertainty and the unexpected in life's affairs . . . the possibility of an accident, even in the most pedestrian activity' (Murphy 1992: 101–102; Longman 1998: 244). But why spend so much effort on stating the obvious? The answer lies in the proverbial string's contextual function. Qoheleth is making a pointedly funny yet subversive point by covertly applying the threat of accidental injury to the strained political situation. When he says *He who digs a pit may fall into it*, he is referring to the foreign regime's insidious role-reversal policy (= the pit!), which, he is implying, will eventually snare them in their own entrapment scheme. When he says *he who breaks down a wall, a snake may bite him*, he is referring to the foreign regime's undoing of social structures (= wall!), which will lead to sudden attack in retaliation (= snake bite!). When he says *He who quarries stones may be injured by them*, he is referring to the foreign regime's exploitative practices (= breaking stones out of their natural environment), which will lead to the *stones* (= Jewish resistance!) harming them in turn. When he says *he who splits logs may be endangered by them*, he is referring to the foreign regime's 'divide and rule' strategy, and he is threatening them with popular resistance. The political pressure and sense of oppression is relieved through veiled allusions which suggest to Qoheleth's audience that they can, after all, do something about their situation. This release from the communal sense of strain creates emotional relief, the genius of political jokes.

10. In verses 10–15, traditional proverbs list lessons to be learned from the observations about 'occupational' risks. The first, in verse 10, presents an example of the successful deployment of wisdom, ostensibly by describing and defending the proper maintenance of tools. The veiled threat gains its edge from the multi-referential quality of the term *barzel*, which can refer to iron as a metal, and to instruments of metal, such as an axe or a sword. A realistic self-assessment and the admission that the Jewish population currently cannot overcome the foreign regime (the iron is *blunt, has lost its edge*) leads to the conclusion that there is only one sensible response to the dilemma: *one will whet it* [the sword!] *and make it sharp and strong again.*

The words *yĕgabber gibbôr* are borrowed straight from the battle-field. Yet they normally prompt translations envisaging the use of a blunt tool: 'one must exercise more strength' (Murphy 1992: 97). In reality, Qoheleth is also talking about mustering armies, the noun *ḥăyālîm* being the normal word for armies and the verb *yĕgabber*, 'to strengthen, fortify', being related to the noun *gibbôr*, which is regularly used to designate soldiers. The phrase calls for the mustering of armies for battle. Ironically, the verse ends with the phrase *and success: wisdom prevails!* Sarcastically, the only thing accepted as a *yîtrôn* without qualification in the entire speech is armed combat with the foreign regime!

11. The second proverb presents an example of the unsuccessful deployment of skill: *If the snake bites because there is no incantation, then there is no success for the master of the tongue.* The statement about snake training needs to take verse 8 into account. There, the 'snake' is not an actual reptile, but a metaphor for the Jewish resistance. Consequently, the snake charmer is not an actual expert in pest control. Rather, the designation *master of the tongue* refers to Greek orators who used their skills as public speakers to win over the Jewish population in order to keep them compliant. Their implicit identification as snake charmers is a slur, and striking consonance – two identical-sounding endings on -*ḥāš* – is employed to hilarious effect, mocking the *master of the tongue* through the skilful deployment of the snake's (= resistance's) own tongue imitating the hissing sound of a snake.

12–14a. The beneficial words of the wise are contrasted with the words of the fool: *The words of a wise man's mouth: favour.*

The strong affirmation of *favour* (*ḥen*) for the words of a wise man contrasts with 9:11. Krüger has proposed an intriguing explanation for this phenomenon. Since the pronominal suffix on *těballě'ennû* (*swallow him*) can be related to the fool (v. 12b), to the *favour* of the wise man (v. 12a) or even to the wise man himself, this means that 'the words of a wise man can lose their effect through the speech of a fool', indicating an 'underlying critique of traditional wisdom' (Krüger 2004: 186). An interpretation of Qoheleth's words against the background of Jewish resistance unravels the mystery: while both halves of verse 12 *sound* traditional as long as the fool is considered the referent of the suffix pronoun in 12b, Qoheleth would have been able to signal that the wise person of 12a was the truly intended referent through intonation, pause and body language. The unexpected, counter-intuitive twist would have surprised, delighted and amused the audience. And while he has them laughing, Qoheleth swiftly tags on a string of other hyperbolic statements about the destructive impact of foolish talk: *To begin with, the words of his mouth are foolish, but in the end his mouth is evil stupidity – and a fool multiplies words!* Qoheleth provides an anatomy of foolish overtalk in situations of armed conflict. Words that initially seem just silly soon turn out to be criminally and dangerously stupid, and fools never know when to stop!

14b. In two final reflections in verses 14b–15, Qoheleth returns to one of his signature themes: human ignorance about the future: *Human beings do not know what is to come.* The verse is a variation on the theme (cf. 6:12 and 8:7). The Jewish population has to cope with and adequately respond to the challenges it encounters with its foreign rulers without the comfort of assured success. The risks are real, and so the question *and what will be after them – who can tell them?* takes on a more ominous tone.

15. The Hebrew literally reads: 'The hard work of fools, she will make him breathless' (cf. 1:8), presenting two grammatical discrepancies in just three words. First, the suffix pronoun on the verb *tĕyaggĕʻennû*, which refers to the second, plural noun *hakkĕsilîm*, is singular. Second, the grammatical gender of the verb is feminine, but its subject *ʻămal* is masculine. Grammatical idio-syncrasies in Ecclesiastes are frequent (Longman 1998: 246–247), but two inconsistencies in three words suggest that the text is corrupt (Fox 1999: 307). A textual reconstruction first suggested by Ehrlich restores a meaning which is in line with the wider context: *ʻămal hakkĕsil mātay yĕyaggĕʻennû, The hard work of the fool, when will it leave him breathless?* (Ehrlich 1968). The answer: *ʼăšer lōʼ-yādaʻ lāleket ʼel-ʻir, When he does not know to walk to a city!* This phrase remains, of course, virtually incomprehensible. Most likely, it is a joke ridiculing the fool. The reflection ends on a humorous yet sombre note. Resistance is risky, and it demands wisdom. Fools are not welcome to join.

Meaning

This segment would not look out of place in Machiavelli's *The Prince* or Sun-tzu's *The Art of War*. It would make a valuable contribution to a handbook for resistance fighters. Here are some practical lessons for modern-day resistance activists: (1) Oppose attempts of the enemy to undermine your legitimate government and authority structures. (2) Use the carefully crafted speeches of skilled speakers to motivate resistance among the population. (3) Use humour. (4) Use the enemy's strategies against them. What Ecclesiastes says here needs to be considered in the light of 8:2–9. Qoheleth's reflections on armed resistance to evil challenge Christian attitudes that prohibit violent opposition to evil on principle.

27. HUMOROUS REFLECTION ON BAD GOVERNANCE (10:16–20)

Context

Following the covert critique of a specific foreign policy, Qoheleth here launches into another verbal attack on the alien overlords. This slapstick-style comical interlude begins with a mock lament for a land suffering from bad governance, paired with a mock celebration of a land benefiting from able governance. A hilarious sketch of lazy people who court disaster by energetically distracting themselves from their responsibilities with frivolous pursuits leads to an insincere prohibition against criticizing such people, in the very act of doing so. This comical interlude provides light relief, releases tensions and aims to take the sting out of the more inflammatory remarks Qoheleth has just made.

Comment

16. In this reflection on bad governance, which unfolds against the background of foreign rule, the opening verse ostensibly expresses sorrow over incompetent government: *Woe to you, O land!* Since there are no clues to the identity of the land, Qoheleth gives the impression that he is engaging in an abstract and hypothetical philosophical reflection. A good number of modern interpreters take Qoheleth at face value (e.g. Murphy 1992: 105). Nonetheless, in Qoheleth's original performances, his actual audience would have heard themselves being addressed, and in the light of prevailing tensions with foreign rulers, an identification with the pitied land would have been natural.

The noun *nāʿar* has two main sets of connotations, 'servant' or 'slave' on the one hand, and 'boy', 'child', 'youth', 'young man' on the other. One meaning signals low social status; the other, young age and immaturity. Qoheleth is, of course, again having fun with a word's multivalence, using the pun in the service of regime-critical doublespeak. When Qoheleth cries *Woe to you, O land!*, he is not only expressing sympathy for a poorly governed land, but he also cries *Woe* over its pathetic king. When he describes this king as a *nāʿar*, he invokes both meanings of the term, giving the impression of an abstract philosophical reflection on unsuitable rulers *and* ridiculing an actual incompetent king's immature behaviour. When he adds *and your leaders feast in the morning*, he is not only complaining about a theoretical scenario, but he also ridicules the actual foreign administration in Judea.

17. When he declares *Happy are you, O land!*, he is not only making a theoretical point about good and legitimate government in general, but he is also casting a vision for a new kind of government for Judea, when they will have taken back control over their land from the foreign intruders. The reference to the king being a son *of the freeborn/of the noble ones* (the Hebrew word *ḥôrim* can refer to both [Koehler, Baumgartner and Stamm 2001: 348]) is therefore a play on words which refers not only to a noble character or high social status ('noble ones'), but also to national independence ('freeborn ones').[1]

18. Probably coined by Qoheleth himself with a side glance at well-known amusing aphorisms like Proverbs 21:9; 25:24; 27:15, this proverb ridicules lazy rulers for wilful dereliction of duty.

---

1. I owe this insight to a personal communication from David Firth, November 2018.

19. Qoheleth follows this with an over-the-top description of their lackadaisical attitudes: *For a laugh they prepare food, and wine makes life joyful, and money is the answer for everything!* This is not only sardonically critical of feasting, debauchery and affluent spending in general, but condemns sets of behaviour that can often be observed when people are put in authority over concerns they do not care about, such as running a foreign country for personal gain and an absentee king's financial benefit, as was the case in Qoheleth's Judea under Ptolemaic rule. The final phrase about the buying power of money exposes the local rulers' cynical incompetence. They justify their neglect of the local population's concerns – and the possible repercussions for themselves – with the illusion that their money, no doubt amassed at the expense of the people, can buy them out of any trouble.

20. Taken at face value, the next statement can be read as a wholesale endorsement of 'conformist and opportunist quietism in political practice' (Krüger 2004: 189; Crüsemann 1984: 71). And this is how Qoheleth wanted his words to be understood by any who might wish him ill.

Numerous indicators, however, suggest that the verse can also be heard as ironically regime-critical. (1) There is the context of the earlier statements in this sequence, especially verse 16 (Fox 1999: 310–311). (2) The statement is exaggeratedly stylized. The offences which he ostensibly warns against – *The king you should not curse . . . you should not curse the rich* – are arranged in chiastic order and are overly repetitive, signalling a stilted sincerity which in reality is anything but. (3) The statement is itself incongruous, for how can the sound of a curse that occurred in one's *thoughts* or in one's bedroom be carried through the air by winged creatures? (4) The overdrawn, fantastical description of possible informants – *for 'a bird from heaven' may carry the sound, or 'the master of the wings' may tell the matter* – suggests that Qoheleth is not thinking of actual winged creatures; rather, he is talking of *human* informants, which he caricatures and ridicules. The unusual designation *the master of the wings* may in fact be an insulting nickname given to a particularly effective informant or to the head of the 'secret service' of the foreign regime. This statement, then, is also meant to be interpreted ironically, as regime-critical (cf. Krüger 2004: 189). In

Qoheleth's verbal strategy the verse was designed to be heard as loyalistic *and* regime-critical, just not by the same people. The verse was meant to be funny, taking the sting out of people's worries over Qoheleth's daring words.

Meaning

This slapstick-style comical interlude is at once one of the funniest and one of the darkest moments in Qoheleth's routine. His insincere prohibition of criticizing such people while in the same breath exposing them to ridicule is a stroke of genius, and it is hilarious.

28. INSTRUCTIONS ON RISK-TAKING (11:1–6)

Context

After the preceding comical interlude, dark yet funny, Qoheleth now comes to the heart of his message. His routine reaches a didactic climax, signalled by the high number of directives – four verb forms with imperatival force in the short space of six verses. The segment provides a snapshot sketch of the internal dialogue in Qoheleth's community about the risks and opportunities involved in their responses to foreign rule. Just below his allusive and underdetermined language, Qoheleth challenges his community to resist foreign demands. He urges them to take decisive action but spread the risks of retaliation. He anticipates internal opposition to his programme and ridicules common objections. He encourages his community with reference to divine intervention on their behalf, and promises rich rewards.

The present segment is a recruitment speech couched in allusive phrases which hide Qoheleth's true intentions. Placed strategically near the end of his routine, it articulates the main purpose of the entire speech: to encourage his audience to resist foreign pressure and to hold on to their traditional way of life. As such, it also prepares the way for the climactic conclusion of his routine.

Comment

1–2. These instructions are metaphorical and underdetermined. Consequently, they have been interpreted in a variety of ways, with three main understandings: (1) as advice on wealth creation in the business world (Longman 1998: 256); (2) as an expression of the paradox that foolish behaviour can succeed while wise conduct may fail (Ringgren and Zimmerli 1981); (3) as an encouragement to charitable giving (so, e.g., Targum, Rashi, Ibn Ezra; and Krüger 2004: 192; Fox 1999: 312).

The term *your bread* does not refer to actual food rations, but it can stand for a range of innocuous things, a clever way of hiding what Qoheleth really means: *your bread* is a cypher for the investment of time and effort which Qoheleth invites his target audience to contribute to the resistance effort. All forms of investment carry risks, and while opposing the foreign regime is the most dangerous form of investment, it is nonetheless worth the effort because Qoheleth's community face risk all the same, whether or not they become involved: *for you do not know what evil may happen on the earth/ against the land.*

3–4. These next claims are humorous wisecracks designed to mimic actual proverbs and lampoon lethargic inertia and apathetic fatalism dressed up in the guise of traditional wisdom. Most scholarly interpretations, nonetheless, take them at face value (Lauha 1978: 201–202; Eaton 1983: 142; but cf. Krüger 2004: 193 n. 9). They fail to catch Qoheleth's dark sense of humour. Rather, Qoheleth here is repeating, for the benefit of his audience, a parody of the arguments of those in the Judean community who counsel caution, perhaps expressing a fatalistic resignation under the influence of a Stoic philosophy promoted by the foreign elites. The claim *in the place where the tree falls, there it will be,* a platitude that sounds as stilted and lame in Hebrew as in modern translation, may indeed reference a fatalistic compliance with whatever political developments the flow and ebb of foreign powers and their rivalries may bring.

5. Likely with the laughs of his audience under his wings following his crack at the internal opposition, Qoheleth now turns to an inspirational fact with which he aims to stir the enthusiasm of the crowd: *Just as you do not know how the breath comes to the bones in the mother's womb, so you do not know the work of God, who makes everything.* He uses the affirmation of human ignorance over the mysterious power of prenatal life to rouse his audience's enthusiasm for the cause. Just as they do not know how the life-breath comes to a child in its mother's womb – one of the most miraculous and life-giving phenomena in the natural world – so they cannot know how God will make the revolutionary cause succeed; and yet God can do it, for the phrase *God, who makes everything* is an intentionally multivalent phrase with three meanings, each as inspiring as the others: it can refer to the God 'who has made everything', to the God 'who is doing everything' and to the God 'who is able to do everything'. In short, Qoheleth implies, if this God, with his unfathomable and unlimited power, is for us, who can be against us?

6. On the basis of this encouraging truth, Qoheleth challenges his audience to take up the cause. The example of sowing seed taken from agriculture stands not only for enterprising activity in general, but also for the many ways in which the Jewish population can resist the foreign occupation. The invitation to industrious activity aims at the promotion of commitment and dedication. The listing of demonstrative pronouns (three times) promotes creativity: there is more than one way of supporting the cause, a detail which takes up the earlier advice in verse 2 to spread the risks. Everybody can do something, and every little helps.

Meaning
This is a snapshot account of one man of God's verbal response to inertia in the face of persistent evil. Inertia is never a good option because ultimately the evil we fail to oppose may eventually find its way to our own door. Qoheleth employs humour. His response is acerbically sarcastic, impatient, and aims to expose the ridiculous nature of inertia in the face of evil. He challenges others to invest themselves in the fight for the common good. He employs inspirational rhetoric, encouraging his community with reference to the supernatural power of God: resistance to evil will inevitably bear fruit.

29. INSTRUCTIONS ON HOW TO ENJOY LIFE FROM BEGINNING TO END (11:7 – 12:7)

Context

Qoheleth's inspiring and motivational climax (11:7 – 12:7) brings his oratory to a rhetorical and didactic culmination. It begins with a beautifully evocative, motivational introduction (11:7), leads into a series of eight instructions on how to maximize happiness from the beginning to the end of life (11:8 – 12:1) and concludes with a motivational meditation on the future, really an allusive and evocative, highly metaphorical description of five impending obstacles to happiness that is characterized by a sense of foreboding and inevitability which adds urgency to these instructions (12:2–7). The resulting instruction is a pastiche of genres, a poetic masterpiece.

Comment

7. The final sequence in Qoheleth's motivational speech opens with an apparently upbeat and motivational observation: the phrase *light is sweet* may simply mean 'life's good!' It is difficult to take this claim as anything other than an entirely positive endorsement of the beauty of life (Krüger 2004: 195), but most commentators still manage to do so (e.g. Longman 1998: 259; Fox 1999: 316–317). The phrase is beautifully evocative, juxtaposing metaphors through a creative mix of synaesthetic experiences.

The remainder of the statement, however, claims that it is *good*, that is, enjoyable and desirable, to *see the sun*. For once, it seems, the sun functions as an emblem for life rather than as a cypher for the foreign regime. However, the statement is also an ironical inversion of what it appears to say: the incongruity created through the mixing of metaphors via the association of light (visual stimulus) with taste (*sweet*, gustatory sensation) suggests that Qoheleth means more than what he says. Reference to the sun also signals that he is talking about the usual suspect, the foreign regime. Therefore, the claim that *it is good for the eyes to see the sun* is in reality an ironical reference to the attraction which power and success typically exert. The *sun* (= the foreign regime) appears attractive only to those who let their judgment be clouded by outward, superficial observation (= the eyes), but in reality it is not good at all from the perspective of Qoheleth's value system, which he continues to impart to his audience. Again Qoheleth confronts his audience and later readers with calculated multivalence. The statement is an inspirationally positive and programmatic heading for what follows; and it is also an ironical comment on the superficial attraction that many fellow Jews feel towards the foreign regime. It prompts no fewer than eight instructions on how to maximize happiness. The two-faced beginning which prompts this, the longest series of instructions in the entire book, alerts us from the start that these instructions may also have more than one meaning.

8. Qoheleth offers and defends two instructions. First, there is the instruction to enjoy life at all times: *So, if a man lives many years, let him rejoice in them all!* Because life is in and of itself good, human beings can and should enjoy every season of their lives, the many years from youth to old age. The verb *rejoice* is an imperfect which can be interpreted as an indicative and as a jussive. Both meanings are intended.

Since a long life includes of necessity many days of darkness, there is both the reality that a person *will* look back on such dark periods in old age *and the instruction to keep in mind* that periods of darkness in our lives are inevitable: *and he will/let him remember the days of darkness, that they, too, will be many!* The ambiguity here, too, is deliberate, and again both meanings are intended (Krüger 2004: 296).

The emphasis on enjoying life when young contests an understanding of life which values longevity over vitality, which promotes patience over authenticity and which suspends integrity in anticipation of an ill-defined future reward. It is against this challenge that the remainder of the verse, which justifies these two instructions, takes on a radically new significance. When Qoheleth claims that *All that is to come is a mirage*, he is not claiming that life has no meaning (contra Longman 1998: 260); rather, he challenges the worldview of those who sympathize with the foreign regime and try to appease the local population with vague promises of a better future.

9. And so the following four instructions develop an alternative vision for the life of the young people in Qoheleth's audience.

In the first instruction, young people are encouraged to seek happiness here and now. In the second instruction, Qoheleth urges the youngster, *and let your heart make you good in the days of your youth!* The idea of a young person's heart making him or her *good* sounds as curious in Hebrew as it does in English translation. Qoheleth personifies the internal organ and invites his young audience to grant to the seat of their critical faculties the permission to 'make them good', an ambiguous phrase which may mean 'make you happy', 'make you well physically' or 'make you morally good'. The evocatively enigmatic nature of the demand has thought-provoking and amusing effect.

For those in the know, the similarity between the third and fourth instructions and Numbers 15:39 was hard to miss. The demand *And follow on the paths of your heart and what your eyes see* seems to fly in the face of ancient Israelite dress code, according to which the tassels on their garments supposedly reminded law-abiding Israelite citizens not to follow 'after their hearts and after their eyes' because these 'organs of desire' would lead them into sin (Krüger 2004: 196; Longman 1998: 261). Qoheleth provocatively plays with his audience's sartorial norms and sense of propriety, to hilarious effect.[1] These instructions are invigorating, liberating and exhilarating, especially for a young audience, then and now. They are not, however, libertarian and hedonistic, as the surrounding statements demonstrate (Krüger 2004: 196; Ogden 1984: 31).

Qoheleth's instruction *know that over all these things God will bring you into judgment* serves as justification for youthful rejoicing. But what is the referent of the phrase *over all these things*? An ingenious ancient explanation is still the best: 'A man must render account for everything he saw but did not enjoy' (*b. Nedarim* 10a). Therefore, the statement is not about posthumous judgment in case Qoheleth's young audience were following their hearts and eyes too much; rather, in line with the this-worldly orientation of divine judgment throughout the Old Testament, divine accountability operates in the here and now, and Qoheleth is provocatively and humorously turning his audience's expectation about divine judgment on its head: God will not condemn them for enjoying themselves too much; he will hold them accountable for not enjoying themselves enough! The effect is hilarious, liberating and energizing.

10. The upbeat, light-hearted tone continues into the next instruction: *And turn vexation away from your heart and remove evil from your body*. As so often in this instructional series, the verse consists of a two-part instruction followed by a justification. Ambiguity prevails, for the instructions can be taken in different ways. First, they can be 'admonitions to live a joyful and apparently carefree life' (Longman 1998: 261). Or they can be ethical instructions to avoid resentful bitterness (*ka'as*) and immoral retaliation (*rā'â*) in response to adverse treatment by others (cf. 5:17 and 7:9). Again, Qoheleth plays with his audience's expectations and consciously prompts both interpretations. On the one hand, he seems to offer a harmless piece of advice consisting of coping strategies for overcoming the irritations of ordinary life. On the other hand, he commends a mature non-violent response to the foreign regime's constant provocations.

---

1. In a later age, when readers missed the joke, the tension between 11:9 and Num. 15:39 provoked debate over the canonicity of the book of Ecclesiastes (see Longman 1998: 26–27, 260).

Qoheleth justifies his admonition with a curious claim: *for youth and black hair are a mirage!* The nouns *youth* and *black hair* are metaphors for youthful arrogance and naïve overconfidence. Qoheleth declares them a mirage not only because they are transient, but also because they can create a self-image of invincibility which may draw young hotheads into violent conflicts with the occupying power. Thus, the point of the justification is not to favour youth over old age, but to motivate behaviour that avoids standard responses to provocation. He is encouraging his audience to find happiness now (Krüger 2004: 197), even while foreign occupation persists, perhaps the ultimate form of resistance to tactics that aimed to undermine the local population's morale.

12:1a. The eighth and final instruction is the climactic admonition in the series, signalled through its position at the end and through the long string of temporal qualifiers (vv. 1b–7) which follow it: *And remember your creator in the days of your youth!* In the majority interpretation (e.g. Murphy 1992: 118), remembering your creator is taken to mean 'recall the fact that you were created so that you remain aware that you must die, and live according to this reality!' However, the word *bôrĕ'ekā*, ostensibly a reference to *your creator*, seems abrupt and out of place here, and the anomalous plural form ('your creators') draws further attention to the circumstance that more is going on. Thus, a number of ingenious emendations have been suggested, the most attractive of which are (1) *bĕ'erkā*, 'your well' (which metaphorically can refer to one's birth and to one's wife); and (2) *bôrĕkā*, 'your pit', a reference to one's grave (Longman 1998: 267). All three of these meanings were already perceived in antiquity:

> A threefold interpretation of the difficult word *bôrĕ'ekā* is attributed
> to Aqiba in explaining the saying of Akabya ben Mahalalel in Abot 3:1
> ('know whence you came' [*b'rk*, your source], 'whither you are going'
> [*bwrk*, 'your grave'], 'and before whom you are destined to give an
> accounting' [*bwryk*, 'your Creator']).
> (Crenshaw 1987: 185)

This ancient interpretation suggests that the word was meant to be a play on words with at least three different meanings from the start, and presumably Qoheleth's live audience would have noticed straight away that Qoheleth was having fun with this word because of his unnatural pronunciation and intonation of it, signalled in writing by the additional letter *yod*. In Qoheleth's spoken delivery, this would have sounded like 'your creators', but he could have signalled through body language and intonation that the sound marking the word as plural did not indicate several creators but several intended meanings of the word. Last but not least, the mention of the word *creator[s]* also provided a hint that the coming metaphorical description in 12:1b–7 was related to the theme of creation, or rather uncreation. Qoheleth challenges his audience to remember their-origin-and-their-creator-and-their-grave, all at once (Krüger 2004: 197; Lohfink 1994).

But what does it mean that Qoheleth urges the young members of his audience to remember their origin/creator/grave *in . . . your youth*? There is virtual unanimity that the temporal qualifiers in 12:1b–7 refer to old age. Consequently, the phrase *in . . . your youth* is usually taken at face value, as simply referring to one's youth (Longman 1998: 267). However, this expression can have several other meanings as well, in line with the polyvalent significance of the poetic description of impending doom in the final words of Qoheleth's speech.

1b. In 12:1b–7 Qoheleth describes five impending obstacles that may prevent his audience from enjoying their lives. These verses are *not* a poem, despite the strong scholarly unanimity on the matter. Rather, they are a collage of verbal images which fire the imagination, then and now.[2]

The images that follow paint a graphic picture reminiscent of eschatological scenarios elsewhere in the Old Testament (e.g. Joel 2:1; Amos 5:18, 20; 6:3; 8:9–11; Mic. 2:4; 3:6). They are structured through the repetition of the ominously prescient temporal reference *when not yet*, suggesting inevitability. The scene envisions a future time when very bad things will occur (Krüger 2004: 201).

---

2. For a review of recent interpretations of 12:1b–7, see Krüger 2004: 198–200.

Differences in detail notwithstanding, Longman sums up well the general consensus: 'the passage presents images evoking dread and sorrow in the light of encroaching old age and impending death' (Longman 1998: 269). By contrast, several features in this verse also suggest poetically veiled references to armed combat on the streets of Jerusalem. They combine to portray a poetically veiled scene of eschatological judgment on the foreign regime and its collaborators.

2. The scenario of all heavenly luminaries and light itself being extinguished is a poetic description of the undoing of creation: *when not yet will have darkened the sun and the light and the moon and the stars* describes an unstoppable future period of complete darkness in which acts of God's creative work will have been undone, the products of God's creative activity on days one and four of creation (Gen. 1:3–5, 14–19). Every important word in Ecclesiastes 12:2a appears in the narrative about these two days of creation.

The words *and the clouds return straight after the rain* are considered obscure by some (Fox 1999: 322), but the vocabulary appears elsewhere in a strategic textual location, the flood story. The word *rain* plays a crucial role in the partial undoing of creation in Genesis 7:12; 8:2, and it appears only here in the entire book of Genesis. The word for *clouds* (*'ābîm*) does not appear at all in Genesis, but its synonym *'ānān*, *cloud*, also appears in the flood story (Gen. 9:13 [3x], 16), and again only here in the entire book of Genesis. This suggests that Qoheleth is alluding to the flood story. He envisions the impending period of disaster as a time of continuous rain, leading to universal destruction.

Finally, the vocabulary of Ecclesiastes 12:2 also appears elsewhere in texts related to eschatological judgment, such as Ezekiel 30:3 and 32:7, both with *'ānān*. Since all the important words or phrases from Ecclesiastes 12:2 appear in Ezekiel 32:7–8, this passage is crucial for our understanding. After Ezekiel is commanded to 'raise a lament over Pharaoh king of Egypt' (Ezek. 32:2), he spends the entire chapter (thirty-two verses!) predicting the destruction of Egypt. The portion of his tirade that echoes Ecclesiastes 12:2b comes in a judgment oracle (Ezek. 32:7–8):

> When I blot you out, I will cover the heavens,
> and make their stars dark;

I will cover the sun with a cloud,
    and the moon shall not give its light.
All the shining lights of the heavens
    I will darken above you,
    and put darkness on your land,
        says the Lord God.

(NRSV)

The intertextual bonds are strong. Qoheleth appropriates words from Ezekiel's judgment oracle against Egypt in order to fabricate a veiled 'oracle' of his own against the Egyptian regime, and he does it so imaginatively that none of the Egyptians would have worked it out, while his Jewish audiences would have got it straight away.

3. Qoheleth describes more closely the anticipated period of widespread terror, thus presenting the third impending obstacle to the completion of his instruction in 12:1a. Despite a broad consensus that these verses describe the decay of the human body as a consequence of old age (e.g. Longman 1998: 270–271; Gordis 1968: 342–344), these verses can also be understood on other levels. For example, they fit the situation of an oncoming storm (Loretz 1964: 191–192) or a household in mourning (Fox 1988). Krüger, by contrast, proposes that these verses describe 'an extraordinary catastrophe that can be interpreted as the judgment of God' (Krüger 2004: 202).

In fact, they describe a city under siege. In line with the quasi-eschatological language of verse 2, the temporal clause *on the day when* (*bayyôm še-*) is Qoheleth's version of the eschatological Day of the Lord in the prophetic literature, usually conveyed through the formulaic *bayyôm hahû'*, 'on that day'. The phrase *the guards of the house tremble* is therefore a reference to fearful watchmen, actual soldiers guarding the city, and the word *house* has replaced the word 'city' in order to obscure the military subtext of the designation and baffle foreign ears. Similarly, the phrase *'anšê heḥāyîl*, usually translated 'and the strong men are bent' (NRSV), literally refers to 'men of the army' (the noun *ḥāyîl* has a range of meanings, but in military contexts most naturally refers to an army) who 'bow down' (= 'surrender'; the *hitpael* indicates that these soldiers bend themselves) before the enemy.

The phrase *and the women who grind cease working* [*ûbāṭlû haṭṭōḥănôt*] *because they are few* [*kî mi'eṭû*] clearly does not refer to the conduct of military personnel. Rather, it reports a scene which, on the face of it, appears to involve the general population in a beleaguered city: women at a public mill. Or so it seems. Apart from the causal particle, every word in this phrase occurs only here in the entire Old Testament. The verb *bṭl* probably means 'to be(come) inactive', 'cease to act' (Koehler, Baumgartner and Stamm 2001: 121). The noun *ṭōḥănā*, referring to female 'grinders', appears only here. Does the plural refer to female millers or to molar teeth (Koehler, Baumgartner and Stamm 2001: 374)? The cognate verb *ṭḥn*, 'to grind', is more frequent. Nonetheless, this statement does not make sense in the real world, irrespective of whether 'grinders' refers to female millers or molar teeth. If the phrase were about molars, then the shortage of teeth in old age would be a nonsensical reason for the abandonment of chewing. With fewer teeth, one has to chew *more*, not less. If the phrase were about actual women at a mill, they would not stop grinding because there were few other women around; rather, they would rejoice over the fact that they did not have to wait for other women, who had come earlier, to finish using the mill. A third possibility presents itself. It fits well with the idea that these verses describe a beleaguered city.

In the context of imminent invasion, ordinary folk tend to flee from the main population centres and disperse into remote rural areas where it is easier to hide. This leaves main cities severely depopulated. Since there are at least two attestations where 'grinding' metaphorically and sarcastically refers to sexual intercourse (Job 31:10; Lam. 5:13), the mention of 'female grinders' here is a sarcastic reference to prostitutes who have remained in the city. They are out of business, because there are 'few strong men' left, with *'anšê heḥāyil*, not *ṭōḥănôt*, serving as the subject for the verb *mi'ēṭû*. This is darkly funny sarcasm.

The next phrase may refer to the fading eyesight of old age (cf. Ps. 69:23; Lam. 5:17), but it also describes a pattern of behaviour common in situations of armed combat: the phrase *and they keep dark when they look through the windows* fits into a situation where people expect danger on the streets outside their homes. It conveys people's natural tendency to keep in the shadow to the side of the window frame when they look outside, in order to avoid attracting unwanted attention, or worse, enemy fire.

4. The description of a city under siege continues. The phrase *when the doors to the street are shut* describes an empty street without the usual street vendors and small makeshift shops that operate from the windows and doors of people's homes. Under the threat of invasion, people have left and, quite literally, shut up shop by closing the doors of their homes that opened on to the streets and which, under normal circumstances, would have served as shop entrances.

The phrase *when the sound of the grinding has fallen*, which appears only here, has been interpreted to describe the loss of hearing or the loss of teeth (Longman 1998: 271). Either identification is problematic. Loss of hearing seems unlikely because the statement is about the production of sound, not its perception. Second, teeth are not usually associated with sound, the topic here and in the following material.

Krüger, by contrast, interprets the phrase against the background of the fall of a house or city in the context of prophetic judgment, with special reference to Jeremiah 25:10, where the banishment of the sound of human joy, the sound of millstones and the light of a lamp are mentioned (Krüger 2004: 202). The statement is about a mill (here singular) producing a softer sound or having fallen silent altogether. Since the sound of moving grindstones is louder when they grind grain rather than when they simply glide past each other empty, the scenario refers to the scarcity of grain and consequent famine in a city under siege.

The phrase *and one rises up at the sound of a bird* is also about sound. Here, however, the concern is with the experience of alarm at the slightest sound, such as the sound of a bird. When the city is depopulated, whole neighbourhoods go quiet, so the slightest sound, such as the sudden call of a vulture or a chicken, may signal danger and cause alarm, prompting people to rise from whatever they are doing to peek outside for fear of impending attack.

The phrase *and all the daughters of song are brought low* can also have several meanings. It may refer to the vocal cords (so already Ibn Ezra), to songbirds or to female singers. Most likely, professional singers hired for a funeral ceremony are in view (Fox 1999: 326).

The multivalence of these phrases is deliberate, and their mysterious quality in this foreboding description is meant to confound easy identification. The numerous and varied interpretations that have been produced demonstrate just how underdetermined this poetic pastiche is, right from the start.

5. Ambiguity also weaves itself through the fourth impending obstacle, which Qoheleth continues to paint with vivid colours but vague contours. First, he announces that this will be a period of terror induced by something tall: *when they are even afraid of what is high*. Does this refer to elderly people being afraid of heights? Possibly; but surely there is more. Qoheleth keeps the identity of the subjects of the plural verb in the shadow. It could be the female singers just mentioned, an entire funeral party, the entire population of a city or all humans on earth. What else might people be afraid of? Fox construes *gābōah* as 'the "High One", that is, God' (Fox 1999: 327). In a besieged city, however, people will be afraid of high structures, such as battle ramparts and siege towers just outside the defensive walls of the city. The phrase *and terrors on the road* also fits the situation of a city under siege, when people keep at home behind closed doors as much as they can, justifiably afraid of what they might encounter outside.

The next phrases list three natural phenomena, each as enigmatic as the others. The meaning of these agricultural metaphors cannot be retrieved with certainty. However, against the context of a city under siege, the blossoming almond tree may be devoured by locusts which grow fat on the agricultural produce because no-one stops their proliferation on the fields surrounding the city, and the caper berries are spoilt where they grow because no-one harvests them (Krüger 2004: 202).

The phrase *because the man is going to his eternal home and the mourners circle on the street* explains that the large number of casualties in the city has caused fear among the populace. The verb 'and they circle' describes the endless cycle of funeral processions as the siege claims one fatality after another. The steadily rising number of the casualties of war is what is causing the widespread terror among the population, not the reality of death as such.

6–7. The sequence ends in a description of the fifth impending obstacle to happiness: violent destruction and human casualties.

The phrase *when not yet has been plundered the silver cord* refers to looting after the besieged city has fallen. The next three phrases describe the violent destruction of household goods and the wilful destruction of property that usually accompany the early phases of a city's violent takeover. In the phrase *and the wheel has not yet been smashed against the cistern*, the noun *galgal* probably does not refer to a pulley similar to those used on top of medieval and modern watering holes in order to lower a bucket into the hole to bring up water from the deep. This technology was not used until later. It is more likely that the wheels of a cart or perhaps even a war chariot were rammed against a cistern in order to make it unusable for the local population. (With the exception of Eccl. 12:6, the noun appears only with reference to the wheels on chariots, which makes it likely that this is the case here, too.) These are not descriptions of natural decay through prolonged use, but of sudden, violent destruction.

The next two phrases evocatively refer to human death, and they apply to death as a result of defeat in war as well as to human mortality in general: *and not yet has returned the dust to the earth, just as it was, and the spirit has not yet returned to God who gave it.* The circumstance that the ominous words *when not yet has . . .* still hover over this beautifully haunting phrase adds an aura of inevitability and finality to the concluding and climactic item in the list of reasons why Qoheleth was urging his audience to remember their origin/creator/grave in their youth. The allusion to Genesis 2:7 is unmistakable, but it describes the reversal of God's actions in the formation (from dust) and animation (through inspiration with the 'breath of life' [*nišmat ḥayyîm*] from God's own lungs, as it were) of humans from dust into God-breathed living beings. As with 12:2, Qoheleth confronts his audience with words that picture uncreation, this time of humans themselves. They are confronted with their own inevitable end, described, quite literally, as the expiration of their spirit – *hārûaḥ*, not *nišmat ḥayyîm* – returning to God who gave it. Is this a *reditus animae ad Deum*, 'the return of the soul to God', as most ancient Christian commentators assumed? With few exceptions (such as Ogden 1987: 207), modern scholars agree that this is not the case (Murphy 1992; Seow 1997; Longman 1998; Fox 1999; Krüger 2004). Qoheleth does not affirm immortality; but this does not mean that he denies it. While he does not imply a continued human existence beyond death, the most important contribution of Qoheleth's final pronouncement is that it forms a powerful theological conclusion to this magnificent prophetopoetic masterpiece, to the inspirational series of instructions on happiness, and to Qoheleth's routine as a whole. And in this conclusion God emerges as the origin and destiny of human life.

Meaning

In the routine as a whole, Qoheleth has consistently reminded his audience of the enduring value of the traditional Jewish way of life. He has also warned against the allure of the attractive foreign ideology, with its apparent invincibility, novel and intriguing belief system, economic success and promise of happiness for those who would support the foreign regime.

At the end of his teaching, Qoheleth first called on his audience to join the resistance (11:1–6). He then gave the longest series of instructions in the entire speech (11:7 – 12:1), in which he presented a series of strategies to maximize happiness within the framework of Jewish beliefs. It is against this background that he now warns his audience that giving in to the foreign regime's allure will render them subject to the eschatological judgment and destruction described in the terrifying scenario of his climactic conclusion.

Qoheleth's public oratory ends with an inspiring invitation to enjoy life to the full within the context of the Jewish faith. Against the reality of impending divine judgment, the final part of Qoheleth's wise teaching is urgent, optimistic and practical. In the process, he presents a 'theology of happiness' in the form of eight instructions. The book as a whole will richly reward careful study with regard to modern ways in which Jewish and Christian believers can live their lives well in the midst of political complexity and material and ideological temptations. In all its complexity, it is full of humour and is a sustained, realistic and practical exploration of how to find true happiness.

30. CONFIRMATION OF THE ORIGINAL HYPOTHESIS (12:8)

Context

The conclusion to Qoheleth's philosophical treatise on human limitations and happiness confirms the hypothesis of the executive summary at the beginning of the speech (1:2): everything, indeed, has been found to be a mirage.

Comment

8. There are two significant formal differences between the final verdict here and the thesis statement at the beginning. First, while the word *qôhelet* appears to have been a personal name or a nickname in 1:2 and throughout the speech, here at the end it appears with the definite article (*haqqôhelet*), signalling its function as a title or professional designation: he is 'the qoheleth', a well-known public speaker. Second, the repeated mirage-statement at the end of the verdict here is much shorter than its counterpart in 1:2. This makes it slightly less emphatic than its equivalent at the beginning of the qoheleth's speech. These slight formal shifts signal a shift in the motto's function (Krüger 2004: 42–44, 206, 256).

Notwithstanding its totalizing formulation, the book's motto is not a pronouncement on all of human reality. Rather, it asserts the essence of Qoheleth's claims about Jewish life *under the sun*, that is, under foreign rule. This was not obvious at the start, but was only and increasingly unfolded through the contours of Qoheleth's spoken word performance. There is a development in the argument of Qoheleth's thought. While the metaphor *hebel* = *mirage* remains constant, the precise impact of the metaphor changes from case to case, and takes on a more and more provocative and confrontational capacity through Qoheleth's speech. What looked like a totalizing statement at the beginning is a radical indictment of the foreign regime and an equally radical challenge to Qoheleth's own community to resist the pressure towards cultural assimilation imposed by the foreign regime. The motto makes one thing clear: 'Whatever stick or carrot the foreign regime may throw at us, it is a mirage!' Here, as the final punchline, it brings the qoheleth's routine to a humorous conclusion.

Meaning
The interpretation of Qoheleth's speech against the sociopolitical, cultural and religious context of Jewish life under foreign rule anchors his message in real life. It also brings out the timeless quality of his message, since the experience of cross-cultural pressures is a constant in human history. Qoheleth's routine deserves to be heard again by modern readers, who are invited to bring their own sociopolitical, cultural and religious experience into dialogue with the powerful words of the ancient orator.

31. EPILOGUE (12:9–14)

Context

The conclusion of the book is an epilogue written several decades after Qoheleth's speech would have been recorded in written form (see comment on 7:27 and 8:2). New circumstances in the epilogist's own time had made Qoheleth's words relevant for a new generation, and so the epilogist reissued Qoheleth's work.

He composed this epilogue in order to commend Qoheleth's original work, similar to the blurb on the cover of a modern book. In order to raise interest, he provides a brief characterization of Qoheleth (vv. 9–10b) and affirms his work's polemical value in metaphorical terms (vv. 10c–11). The epilogue concludes with two admonitions that summarize its significance (vv. 12–14): he warns against rival publications (v. 12), summarizes the message of the book (v. 13) and commends this message to his readers (v. 14).

The textual evidence suggests that there is only one epilogue (Longman 1998: 274). It does not significantly alter or critique Qoheleth's original words; rather, it accurately summarizes (and thereby of necessity simplifies) the essence of Qoheleth's intention

(Limburg 2006: 125). And it applies it to the epilogist's own situation of religious, cultural and political tensions with a new foreign regime which now occupies Judea. The current regime, however, works under a new set of policies leading to more repressive and provocative actions that will eventually cause Jewish resentment to boil over and lead to open revolt. It is likely that the book of Ecclesiastes played an important role in these developments.

Comment

9. A short phrase signals that the epilogist is expanding on Qoheleth's work: *But there was more to him* (*wĕyōter šehāyâ*). The editor commends Qoheleth as a gifted and influential speaker from the recent past. First, he claims that *Qoheleth was a wise man*. With this label, the editor puts his author into a class of people who were highly respected in Jewish society. Second, he offers two brief but significant comments on Qoheleth's main professional activities. On the one hand, *he also taught the people knowledge*. This detail commends Qoheleth's concern for public education. For all its brevity, this is an astute observation on what Qoheleth has been doing in 1:3 – 12:7. He had played an important role in educating his own generation in a situation where loyalty to their ancient traditions and religious values was crucial. And by implication, his words are accessible to the average person in the epilogist's own time, too. On the other hand, we are informed, *he heard, selected and arranged many proverbs*. This statement links Qoheleth with other collectors of proverbial wisdom, such as King Solomon (Prov. 1:1; 10:1) and King Hezekiah's editors of Solomonic proverbs (Prov. 25:1), and it anticipates the reference to *masters of collections* a few words later. Qoheleth is characterized as a person of great learning, well versed in the nation's traditional wisdom and able to reflect critically on its significance and benefit for the people.

10a. The reader learns that Qoheleth worked hard in the preparation of his public performances. The phrase *Qoheleth sought to find* signals intense preparatory work. What Qoheleth was working for so carefully is revealed through the phrase *dibrê-ḥepeṣ*, usually translated *pleasing words*. This is a surprising designation for what the editor's readers will find in the written record of Qoheleth's words. Qoheleth's words are in reality difficult, critical and provocative.

It is unlikely that the editor used the word *ḥepeṣ* in the same way that Qoheleth did (e.g. 3:1). Rather, the editor commends Qoheleth's intention to entertain, to find ways of presenting his message in attractive ways. It is also possible that the editor still perceived and appreciated the humorous side of Qoheleth's routine. In that case, perhaps the editor was saying: 'and he worked hard to be funny'.

10b. Qoheleth's editor turns to a commendation of the work itself: *and what is written [here] is correct; [these are] words of truth.* The editor proudly presents his new edition by extolling its virtues. The editor affirms that Qoheleth's work authentically speaks to the issues it sought to address. His words are *words of truth* in the sense that they are realistic, true to life, appropriate to the living conditions *under the sun*, the same *sun* that is still shining, with even greater intensity, in the epilogist's own time.

11. The statement *Words of the wise are like the goads* places Qoheleth's work into a genre with the words of other wise people, such as the book of Proverbs. The statement metaphorically describes the effect of such words in terms of farming equipment used to control particularly large and powerful animals, such as oxen (cf. 1 Sam. 13:21), which are not easily controlled. The next phrase, *and the masters of collections are like fixed nails*, most likely continues the farming imagery, since the following phrase, that they *are given by one shepherd*, mentions someone who looks after livestock. What do these metaphors mean? Three things in the two similes are clear: both are instruments of the shepherd to coerce strong and wilful herd animals to follow his lead; both are painful; and both are presumably applied for the animals' ultimate benefit, despite the inflicted pain. The main intended meaning is to exonerate Qoheleth as an ultimately benevolent 'shepherd', despite the challenging and often uncomfortable nature of his work.

There is an ancient and venerable tradition of understanding the phrase *given by one shepherd* as a reference to God. Many modern interpreters reject this notion (Fox 1999: 355–356). It is also not clear whether it is *the wise* and *the masters* who are given by the shepherd, or whether it is their *words* and their *collections*, or both.

Either way, the designation does not refer to an actual sheep-herder. It must refer to someone who has the capacity to provide either wise words or masterful collections, or it must refer to someone who can provide authors of such words or collections. It seems unlikely that *only* a human referent is in view, for several reasons.

First, those who provide words and collections are a group of people, not one (*'eḥād*). Second, someone who could provide wise and masterful authors of wise words or compilers of collections would have to be a 'master of masters' and/or a person of superior wisdom to foster such expertise among his students. While Qoheleth just about fits this criterion, a reference to God, unusual as it seems, is at least as likely. In conclusion, the reference to the *one shepherd* is intentionally ambiguous. Both references are intended, and, by implication, Qoheleth's editor is making a veiled claim for Qoheleth's words to be divinely inspired, the highest commendation he can give to his new edition of Qoheleth's original work.

Third, the extremely rare term *'ăsuppôt*, plural for *'ăsuppah*, a noun derived from the verb *'sp*, 'to gather, collect', may indicate that Qoheleth's editor is talking about more than a group of wisdom collections (Koehler, Baumgartner and Stamm 2001: 75). The term occurs nowhere else in the Old Testament, but its derivation from the popular verb *'sp* ensures its transparency in terms of surface meaning. Its lack of attestation elsewhere suggests that it may be an original coinage by Qoheleth's editor himself, perhaps in response to a situation where the collective of traditional Jewish literature is confronted with an alternative body of texts that challenges its popularity among the Jewish population.

It appears, then, that the editor is talking about a *collection of writings*, a library, as it were, of traditional Jewish works. This collection clearly included Qoheleth's original work, but it would also have included other popular works, including the religious writings held sacred by contemporary Jewish believers.

The *shepherd*, namely Qoheleth, is identified as one of the masters of collections and thus as a fixed nail. And he is also identified as one of the wise, whose words are *goads*. Behind it all, however, is divine providence. What the shepherd gives, then, are collected wise words, the teaching contained in the book of Ecclesiastes as reissued by the epilogist. This concludes the editor's comments on the author and his work, and the editor now turns to address his intended readers with two closing instructions.

12. His concluding instructions are introduced with the second occurrence of the appendix marker, *And there is more* (*wĕyōter*). It indicates that the epilogist now turns to the second and final part of his editorial comments. The term also signals a change in tone from description to prescription.

What follows is a warning against rival publications, supported with two observations. This forewarning is phrased in traditional instructional language, using the address *my son* to personalize the didactic lesson, although the editor was, of course, hoping for a wider readership.

The phrase *Of making many books there is no end* is clearly polemical, betraying the editor's exasperation with the apparently endless production of new literature *beyond these*, that is, texts beyond the Jewish classics (Lohfink 1994). Other interpretations are possible (Longman 1998: 281; Krüger 2004: 212), but Qoheleth's editor follows his literary hero's strategy of hiding his true intentions, very likely for the same reasons that prompted Qoheleth's original scheme: plausible deniability. The phrase *Of making many books* indicates that the editor is talking about 'the whole spectrum of dealing with books' (Krüger 2004: 212). The over-the-top hyperbole aims to discredit the influx of new literature which the editor clearly resents. But what kind of literature is he talking about? The answer to this question is implicit in the next phrase, the editor's second motivation for his warning to abstain from it and rather focus on writings like Qoheleth's.

The phrase *and excessive study leads to breathlessness of flesh* is strange, on any interpretation (but cf. 1:18). The phrase is often taken to warn the son from studying other wisdom books. However, this seems unexpected in conjunction with the editor's earlier commendation of wise sayings and collections of proverbs. More likely, then, another body of literature is in view, a library of foreign literature, to be precise (Plumptre 1898; Barton 1908: 198–199). The text's silence on the rejected literature's provenance is precisely the point. For reasons of plausible deniability, the editor only hints at what he really means.

This brings us to the curious note that, according to the editor, it is the *body* that becomes breathless (*yĕgi'at bāśār*) through excessive study (cf. 1:8; 10:15). The connection between intellectual inquiry through reading and physical exertion suggests an allusion to the gymnasium, an

> ancient Greek institution devoted to physical education and development
> of the body [*gumnos*, 'naked']. Although originally established for
> functions of a purely athletic and competitive nature, the gymnasium
> eventually became dedicated to the furthering of intellectual, as well
> as physical, aspects of Greek culture.
> (Gafni 2008: 160)

This fits well into the historical events recorded in 2 Maccabees 4:7–15; 6:1–11; and 1 Maccabees 1:10–59.

In conclusion, the dramatic events of 175–160 BC, with the establishment of a gymnasium in Jerusalem and the pursuit of repressive policies aiming at a forced Hellenization of the Jewish population under the Seleucid King Antiochus IV Epiphanes, fit very well with verses 11–12. While impossible to demonstrate with certainty, it is extremely likely that the decades leading up to and perhaps including the dramatic events recorded in 2 Maccabees 4 and 1 Maccabees 1 provided the stimulus for the reissue of Qoheleth's work and the composition of its appendix.

13–14. In a final instruction, the editor presents his summary of Qoheleth's work, introduced with the phrase *The end of the matter* or 'a final word' (*sôp dābār*). The phrase *all has been heard* may signal that Qoheleth's editor was aware of the work's origin as a spoken routine.

The next phrase presents the actual summary, in the form of two complementary instructions: *God you shall fear, and his commandments you shall keep*. The unusual word order puts strong emphasis on the objects, God and his commandments. The emphasis is polemical, implying alternative claims. Reflecting the standard biblical view of human obligation towards God, these directives give a genuine summary of Qoheleth's teaching (contra Crenshaw 1987: 192; Longman 1998: 282; Murphy 1992: 126), for the editor's summary interpretation repeats key statements from the body of Qoheleth's speech (3:14; 5:7; 7:18; 8:12–13) and agrees fully with the interpretations of Qoheleth's speech sequence presented in this commentary (see also Seow 2001: 396).

The epilogue concludes with two motivations for the recommended action: *for this is the whole of every human being, for every deed God will bring into judgment over its hidden motives, whether good or evil.* Faith and obedience are motivated with the warning that people's actions and their hidden motives will be subject to divine scrutiny, in the form of reward or punishment. In the light of the epilogue's late origin, it is possible that the epilogist thinks of posthumous judgment.

Meaning

The epilogue to the book of Ecclesiastes claims that Qoheleth's original words were divinely inspired. As such, it has played an important role in the book's reception as Scripture, in Judaism and in Christianity.

The special contribution of the book as it has been interpreted in this commentary is that it speaks into the sociopolitical, economic and religious complexities of real life, then and now. Much of its teaching is clandestine and intentionally concealed from those who fail to appreciate its explosive, regime-critical purpose. A failure to appreciate its sense of humour and the satirical techniques employed throughout will lead to a limited understanding of the book's message, with only its surface meaning taken into account.

The epilogue indicates that in the first phase of its reception, Qoheleth's explosive didactic programme was still understood and skilfully reutilized under similar circumstances.

The interpretation offered in the present commentary has the capacity to salvage the book from its reception as a merely theoretical reflection on the complexities of life and to recapture it as a scriptural resource which has the power to inspire new generations of Jewish and Christian believers to remain faithful to the essential demands of their faith, to resist the coercion of empire and the temptation of affluence, and to discover true happiness and fulfilment in the process.